Better Homes and Gardens®

# easy quilt projects

Favorites from the Editors of *American Patchwork & Quilting*®

WILEY

John Wiley & Sons, Inc.

Published by John Wiley & Sons, Inc., Hoboken, New Jersey
Published simultaneously in Canada

For general information about our other products and services, please contact our Customer Care Department within the United States at (800) 762-2974, outside the United States at (317) 572-3993 or fax (317) 572-4002.

Wiley also publishes its books in a variety of electronic formats. Some content that appears in print may not be available in electronic books. For more information about Wiley products, visit our web site at www.wiley.com.

ISBN 978-0-470-55931-4

Printed in the United States of America

10 9 8 7 6 5 4 3 2

# contents

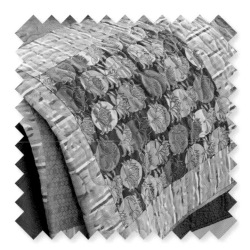

## easy does it
4-59

*Start your quilting adventure with these stunning beginner projects.*

## in the kitchen
60-89

*Spice up a table, pack up your groceries, and serve meals in style.*

## carry on
90-117

*Express yourself with totes, bags, and purses for every occasion.*

## welcome!

There's so much to be excited about when it comes to quilting today. Perhaps it's the stunning fabrics in contemporary patterns, the appeal of an escape after a busy day, or the reward of making something beautiful for yourself or as a gift.

Whatever your reason for quilting, inside this book you'll find ideas to satisfy your creative needs. Packed with easy projects, clever ideas, and clear steps, we hope you'll turn to this collection again and again.

Happy Quilting!

## gifted touches
118-153

*Share your love for quilting with these thoughtful gift-giving ideas.*

## more favorites
154-191

*Try your hand at these hand-picked favorites with modern flair.*

## back to basics
192-208

*Check out the answers to your quilting questions in this guide.*

# easy does it

Are you ready to start quilting but feel short on skill, experience, or time? Jumpstart your quilting with these harder-than-they-look throws and bed quilts and be on the road to completion in no time.

**Ease Into Autumn**............................ 6
**In the Meadow** ............................. 10
**Triangle Tango** ............................. 14
**Make Your Point**........................... 19
**Spice It Up** ................................. 24
**Four Square** ................................ 28
**Slumber Party**.............................. 33
**Puzzle Play** ................................ 40
**Square Off** ................................. 46
**Around the Block**.......................... 51
**Red-and-White Delight**.................. 56

# ease into autumn

DESIGNER **TARA LYNN DARR**
PHOTOGRAPHS **GREG SCHEIDEMANN**

This showcase for fall-tone fabrics
is fast to cut and quick to piece.

*Designer Tara Lynn Darr likes to make scrappy quilts, and for this
beginner project she chose the border fabric first and made her
selections for the blocks based on the color scheme of the border.*

## materials

- 5 yards total assorted dark red, brown, and tan prints (blocks, setting squares)
- 1¾ yards total assorted light prints (blocks, setting triangles)
- ½ yard red print (inner border)
- 3 yards red-and-brown print (outer border, binding)
- 8 yards backing fabric
- 95×103" batting

Finished quilt: 88¾×97⅛"
Finished block: 8" square

Quantities are for 44/45"-wide, 100% cotton fabrics. Measurements include ¼" seam allowances. Sew with right sides together unless otherwise stated.

## cut fabrics

Cut pieces in the following order.

**From assorted dark red, brown, and tan prints, cut:**
- 28—2½×42" strips
- 42—8½" setting squares

**From assorted light prints, cut:**
- 4—2½×42" strips
- 6—13⅜" squares, cutting each diagonally twice in an X to make 24 setting triangles total (you will use 22)
- 2—7" squares, cutting each in half diagonally to make 4 corner triangles total

**From red print, cut:**
- 8—1½×42" strips for inner border

**From red-and-brown print, cut:**
- 9—8×42" strips for outer border
- 10—2½×42" binding strips

## assemble blocks

Referring to **Diagram 1**, sew together four assorted dark red, brown, tan, and light print 2½×42" strips to make a strip set. Press seams in one direction. Repeat to make eight strip sets total. Cut strip sets into 30 8½"-wide Rail Fence blocks total.

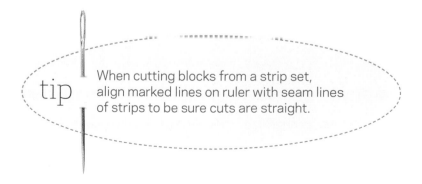

tip — When cutting blocks from a strip set, align marked lines on ruler with seam lines of strips to be sure cuts are straight.

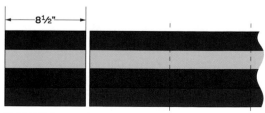

8½"

**DIAGRAM 1**

tip Seams don't match? Did you square up your blocks? If so, and the blocks still don't line up in rows, take the time to remove stitching and rejoin blocks until seams do match.

**QUILT ASSEMBLY DIAGRAM**

**DIAGRAM 2**

**DIAGRAM 3**

## assemble quilt center

[**1**] Referring to **Quilt Assembly Diagram**, lay out Rail Fence blocks, 42 assorted dark red, brown, and tan print setting squares, and 22 assorted light print setting triangles in diagonal rows. In each diagonal row, match up one straight edge of setting triangle with one edge of setting square (**Diagram 2**). A corner of each setting triangle will extend past an edge of the setting square.

[**2**] Sew together pieces in each row. Press seams in one direction, alternating direction with each row.

[**3**] Referring to **Quilt Assembly Diagram**, trim points of setting triangles even with each row's long edges. Join rows; press seams in one direction.

[**4**] At upper left-hand corner and lower right-hand corner of joined rows, trim setting triangles even with edge of setting square (**Diagram 3**).

[**5**] Add light print corner triangles to make quilt center. Press seams toward corner triangles. Trim quilt center to 71¾×80⅛" including seam allowances.

## add borders

[1] Cut and piece red print 1½×42" strips to make:
- 2—1½×80⅛" inner border strips
- 2—1½×73¾" inner border strips

[2] Join long inner border strips to long edges of quilt center. Add short inner border strips to remaining edges. Press all seams toward inner border.

[3] Cut and piece red-and-brown print 8×42" strips to make:
- 2—8×88¾" outer border strips
- 2—8×82⅛" outer border strips

[4] Join short outer border strips to long edges of quilt center. Add long outer border strips to remaining edges to complete quilt top. Press all seams toward outer border.

## finish quilt

[1] Layer quilt top, batting, and backing; baste. (For details, see Quilt It, *page 197.*)

[2] Quilt as desired. This quilt was machine-quilted with a leaf design across the quilt top.

[3] Bind with red-and-brown print binding strips. (For details, see Better Binding, *page 206.*)

**tip** If your quilting is more than 1" from the outer edges, baste the layers together around the quilt ⅜" from the edges. This will prevent the outside edges from ruffling and stretching as the binding is applied.

# in the
# meadow

QUILTMAKER **MABETH OXENREIDER**
PHOTOGRAPHS **CAMERON SADEGHPOUR**

As summer's lush green grasses give way to autumn's blazing leaves and golden skies, create a quilt capturing the season's best colors.

*Start with a green print square, surround it with four mix-and-match rectangles, and voilà—one block is done. Make a block or two each day, and soon you'll have enough for the stunning quilt top. Having no borders to cut and sew lends another fast twist to this project.*

## materials

- 2¾ yards total assorted red prints (blocks)
- 1½ yards total assorted green prints (blocks)
- 2⅝ yards total assorted yellow prints (blocks)
- ¾ yard dark red print (binding)
- 6¾ yards backing fabric
- 79×95" batting

Finished quilt: 72½×88½"
Finished block: 8" square

**Quantities** are for 44/45"-wide, 100% cotton fabrics.
**Measurements** include ¼" seam allowances. Sew with right sides together unless otherwise stated.

## cut fabrics

Cut pieces in the following order.

**From assorted red prints, cut:**
- 100—2½×8½" rectangles
- 100—2½×4½" rectangles

**From assorted green prints, cut:**
- 99—4½" squares

**From assorted yellow prints, cut:**
- 98—2½×8½" rectangles
- 98—2½×4½" rectangles

**From dark red print, cut:**
- 9—2½×42" binding strips

## assemble blocks

[1] Referring to **Block Assembly Diagram**, sew assorted red print 2½×4½" rectangles to opposite edges of an assorted green print 4½" square. Press seams toward rectangles.

**BLOCK ASSEMBLY DIAGRAM**

**tip** Begin each project with a new sewing machine needle, or change it after every eight hours of sewing. A blunt needle can weaken fabric or cause skipped stitches.

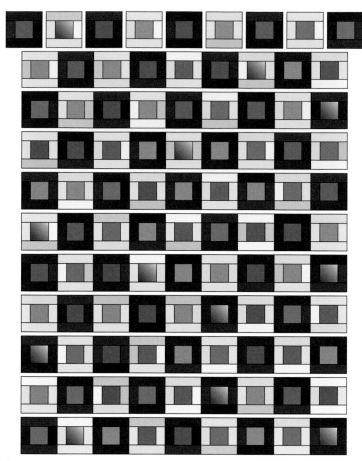

**QUILT ASSEMBLY DIAGRAM**

[2] Join assorted red print 2½×8½" rectangles to remaining edges of green print square. Press seams toward rectangles to make a red block. The red block should be 8½" square including seam allowances.

[3] Repeat steps 1 and 2 to make 50 red blocks total.

[4] Using assorted yellow print rectangles and green print squares, repeat steps 1 and 2 to make 49 yellow blocks total.

## assemble quilt top

[1] Referring to **Quilt Assembly Diagram**, lay out blocks in 11 rows, alternating red and yellow blocks.

[2] Sew together blocks in each row. Press seams in one direction, alternating direction with each row.

[3] Join rows to make quilt top. Press seams in one direction.

## finish quilt

[1] Layer quilt top, batting, and backing; baste. (For details, see Quilt It, *page 197.*)

[2] Quilt as desired. This quilt was machine-quilted with floral and diamond motifs in the block centers. Echo-quilting was added around each center square to add the geometric lInes.

[3] Bind with dark red print binding strips. (For details, see Better Binding, *page 206.*)

## color option

An assortment of pink, purple, and green batiks were used to create this version of In the Meadow. To add a softer touch, sprinkle a few pretty coordinating prints among the batiks.

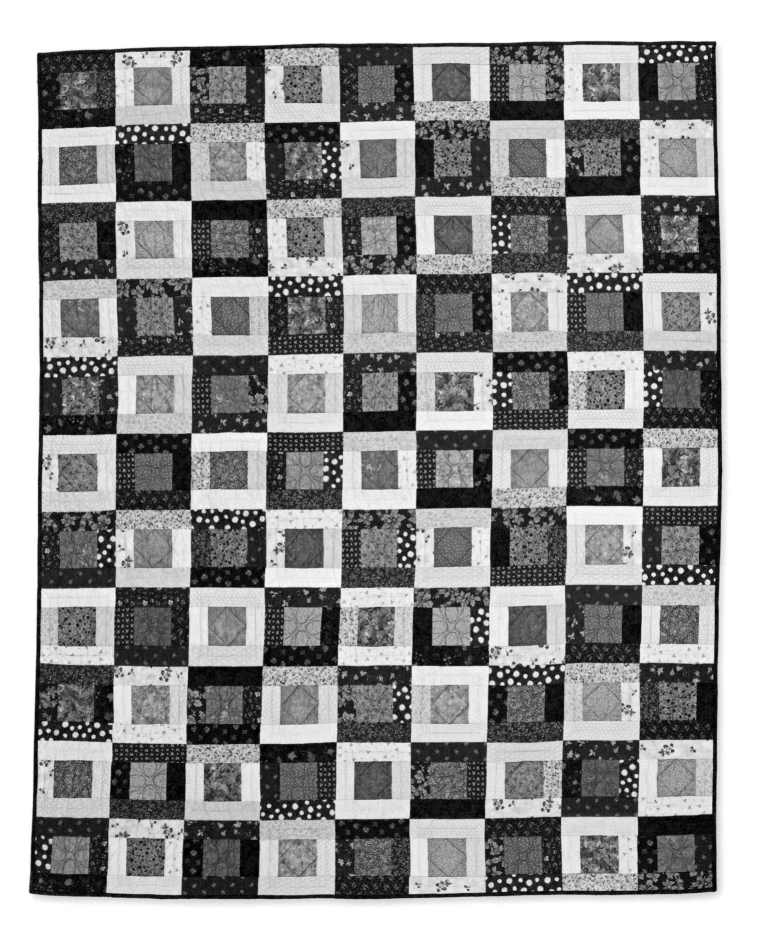

# triangle tango

DESIGNER **ROSEANN MEEHAN KERMES**
PHOTOGRAPHS **GREG SCHEIDEMANN**

Bring on the brights with this easier-than-it-looks queen-bed-size quilt made of half-square triangles.

*The piecing is fast—simply set the matching, high-contrast fabrics in each triangle-square edge-to-edge (not a single diamond to piece in this quilt). Add inner and outer borders, and voilà, you have a finished quilt top ready to be quilted. Designer Roseann Meehan Kermes took her inspiration from the fresh prints of Paisley Party by Terry Atkinson and Liz Lois for Red Rooster.*

## materials

- 2¾ yards white print (blocks)
- 1¾ yards total assorted yellow prints (blocks)
- 1¾ yards total assorted green, blue, and orange prints (blocks)
- ½ yard orange stripe (inner border)
- 1¾ yards aqua floral (outer border)
- ¾ yard yellow geometric print (binding)
- 8 yards backing fabric
- 93×105" batting

Finished quilt: 87×99"
Finished block: 6×12"

Quantities are for 44/45"-wide, 100% cotton fabrics. Measurements include ¼" seam allowances. Sew with right sides together unless otherwise stated.

**tip** Using a design wall or large flat surface makes laying out this quilt a breeze. Offset same-color blocks in each row to make diagonal bands of color across the quilt top.

## cut fabrics

Cut pieces in the following order.

**From white print, cut:**
- 84—6⅞" squares

**From assorted yellow prints, cut:**
- 42—6⅞" squares

**From assorted green, blue, and orange prints, cut:**
- 42—6⅞" squares

**From orange stripe, cut:**
- 8—1¾×42" strips for inner border

**From aqua floral, cut:**
- 9—6½×42" strips for outer border

**From yellow geometric print, cut:**
- 10—2½×42" binding strips

## assemble blocks

[1] Use a pencil to mark a diagonal line on wrong side of each white print 6⅞" square. (To prevent fabric from stretching as you draw the lines, place 220-grit sandpaper under each square.)

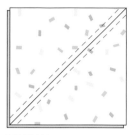
DIAGRAM 1

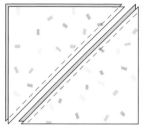
DIAGRAM 2

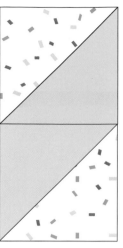
DIAGRAM 3

[2] Layer a marked square atop a yellow, green, blue, or orange print 6⅞" square. Sew together with two seams, stitching ¼" on each side of drawn line (Diagram 1).

[3] Cut joined squares apart on drawn line to make two triangle units (Diagram 2). Press each triangle unit open, pressing seam away from white print, to make two matching triangle-squares. Each triangle-square should be 6½" square including seam allowances.

[4] Referring to Diagram 3, sew together triangle-squares to make a diamond block. Press seam in one direction. The block should be 6½×12½" including seam allowances.

[5] Repeat steps 2-4 to make 84 diamond blocks total.

## assemble quilt center

[1] Referring to Quilt Assembly Diagram, lay out diamond blocks in seven horizontal rows, alternating yellow blocks with green, blue, and orange blocks.

[2] Sew together blocks in each row. Press seams in one direction, alternating direction with each row.

QUILT ASSEMBLY DIAGRAM

[3] Join rows to complete quilt center. Press seams in one direction. The quilt center should be 72½×84½" including seam allowances.

## add borders

[1] Cut and piece orange stripe 1¾×42" strips to make:
- ‣ 2—1¾×84½" inner border strips
- ‣ 2—1¾×75" inner border strips

[2] Sew long inner border strips to long edges of quilt center. Add short inner border strips to remaining edges. Press all seams toward inner border.

[3] Cut and piece aqua floral 6½×42" strips to make:
- ‣ 4—6½×87" outer border strips

[4] Sew outer border strips to long edges of quilt center. Add remaining outer border strips to remaining edges to complete quilt top. Press all seams toward outer border.

## color option

Using a group of whimsical children's prints, such as the Me & My Sister's Butterfly Fling collection for Moda Fabrics, designer Roseann Meehan Kermes seized the chance to use the versatile units from Triangle Tango to make an appealing baby quilt. Roseann sewed together 63 triangle-squares and omitted the borders to make this 42½×54½" quilt. Or change the fabrics to a more sophisticated palette—the generous size makes a cozy throw for grown-ups.

## finish quilt

[1] Layer quilt top, batting, and backing; baste. (For details, see Quilt It, *page 197*.)

[2] Quilt as desired. Machine-quilter Cindy Kujawa stitched a stipple design in the white print areas and outer border. She quilted wavy parallel lines in each colored diamond using matching thread.

[3] Bind with yellow geometric print binding strips. (For details, see Better Binding, *page 206*.)

# make your
# point

Sewing stripes has never been easier!
This quilt comes together quickly with
rows of good-size squares set on point.

*Subdued fabrics flavor row upon row of alternating chevrons in this showy quilt. Stripes meld to make crisp points, and simple floral squares and paisley triangles frame the blocks with a deeper brown.*

## materials

- 1¼ yards brown floral (setting squares)
- 1¼ yards brown paisley (setting and corner triangles)
- ¾ yard brown diagonal stripe (binding)
- 12—18×22" pieces (fat quarters) assorted dark stripes (blocks)
- 10—18×22" pieces (fat quarters) assorted light stripes (blocks)
- 4⅞ yards backing fabric
- 79×87" batting

Finished quilt: 73×80¾"
Finished block: 5½" square

Quantities are for 44/45"-wide, 100% cotton fabrics. Measurements include a ¼" seam allowance. Sew with right sides together unless otherwise stated.

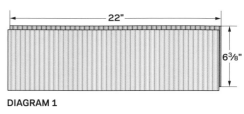

**22"**

**6⅜"**

**DIAGRAM 1**

## cut fabrics

To make the best use of your fabrics, cut pieces in the following order. If you select a lengthwise stripe fabric for binding and would like to have it look like the diagonal-print binding on this quilt, cut 2½"-wide bias strips from a 31" square of fabric (for details, see Cutting on the Bias, *page 203*).

**From brown floral, cut:**
- 34—6" squares

**From brown paisley, cut:**
- 9—11½" squares, cutting each diagonally twice in an X for 36 setting triangles total (you'll use 34)
- 2—7¼" squares, cutting each in half diagonally for 4 corner triangles total

**From brown diagonal stripe, cut:**
- 8—2½×42" binding strips

## assemble chevron blocks

[1] With right sides together, fold a dark-stripe 18×22" piece in half lengthwise to make a 9×22" rectangle. Note: Try folding your fat quarter so just a bit of the bottom layer extends at the top—this makes matching stripes easy.

[2] After making sure stripes on each layer are aligned, cut two 6⅜×22" strips from the folded rectangle (Diagram 1).

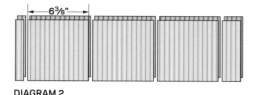

DIAGRAM 2

  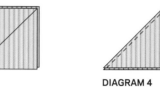

DIAGRAM 3

DIAGRAM 4

[3] Cut layered strips into three sets of layered 6⅜" squares (Diagram 2).

[4] Cut each set of layered squares in half diagonally to make six sets of matching layered triangles (Diagram 3). Keep each set of triangles together; each set will make one chevron block.

[5] Sew together a set of matching triangles along long bias edge to make a chevron block (Diagram 4). When stitching, take care to avoid stretching the bias edges.

[6] Press triangles together as sewn to set seam, then carefully press top triangle open to make a dark chevron block. The block should be 6" square including seam allowances.

[7] Repeat steps 1 through 6 to make 72 dark chevron blocks total.

[8] Using light stripe 18×22" pieces, repeat steps 1 through 6 to make 56 light chevron blocks total.

## assemble quilt top

[1] Referring to **Quilt Assembly Diagram**, lay out dark and light chevron blocks, 34 brown floral 6" setting squares, and 34 brown paisley setting triangles in diagonal rows. Note: Arrange your blocks so all dark chevron blocks point in one direction, and all light chevron blocks point in the other.

[2] Sew together pieces in each row. Press seams in one direction, alternating direction with each row.

[3] Referring to **Quilt Assembly Diagram**, trim points of setting triangles even with each row's long edges. Join rows to make quilt top. Press seams in one direction.

[4] At lower left-hand corner and upper right-hand corner of quilt top, trim setting triangles even with the edge of the setting square (Diagram 5).

[5] Add brown paisley corner triangles to corners of quilt top. Press seams toward corner triangles.

## finish quilt

[1] Layer quilt top, batting, and backing; baste. (For details, see Quilt It, *page 197.*)

[2] Quilt as desired. This quilt features an allover feather design stitched across the quilt.

[3] Bind with brown diagonal-stripe binding strips. (For details, see Better Binding, *page 206.*)

DIAGRAM 5

**QUILT ASSEMBLY DIAGRAM**

tip — To keep stripes straight and reduce shifting, press folded layers of fabric together before cutting.

# spice it up

QUILTMAKER **KATHLEEN WILLIAMS**
PHOTOGRAPHS **GREG SCHEIDEMANN**

This cozy throw packs a visual punch because of the zesty large floral, 14½"-finished squares and eye-popping sashing.

*There's little doubt that the fabric makes the quilt when you showcase spunky prints in the simplest of quilt designs. A selection of floral and striped prints combine to make this dramatic, contemporary quilted throw.*

## materials

- 1½ yards orange floral (squares)
- 1½ yards mottled orange (squares)
- ⅝ yard mottled green (sashing squares)
- 2¼ yards orange stripe (sashing)
- ⅔ yard mottled teal blue (binding)
- 4⅞ yards backing fabric
- 67×86" batting

Finished quilt: 61×79¾"

Quantities are for 44/45"-wide, 100% cotton fabrics. Measurements include ¼" seam allowances. Sew with right sides together unless otherwise stated.

## cut fabrics

To make the best use of your fabrics, cut pieces in the following order.

**From orange floral, cut:**
- 6—15" squares

**From mottled orange, cut:**
- 6—15" squares

**From mottled green, cut:**
- 20—4¾" sashing squares

**From orange stripe, cut:**
- 31—4¾×15" sashing rectangles

**From mottled teal blue, cut:**
- 8—2½×42" binding strips

tip — Adhere small sandpaper dots to the underside of your ruler to prevent it from slipping while rotary cutting.

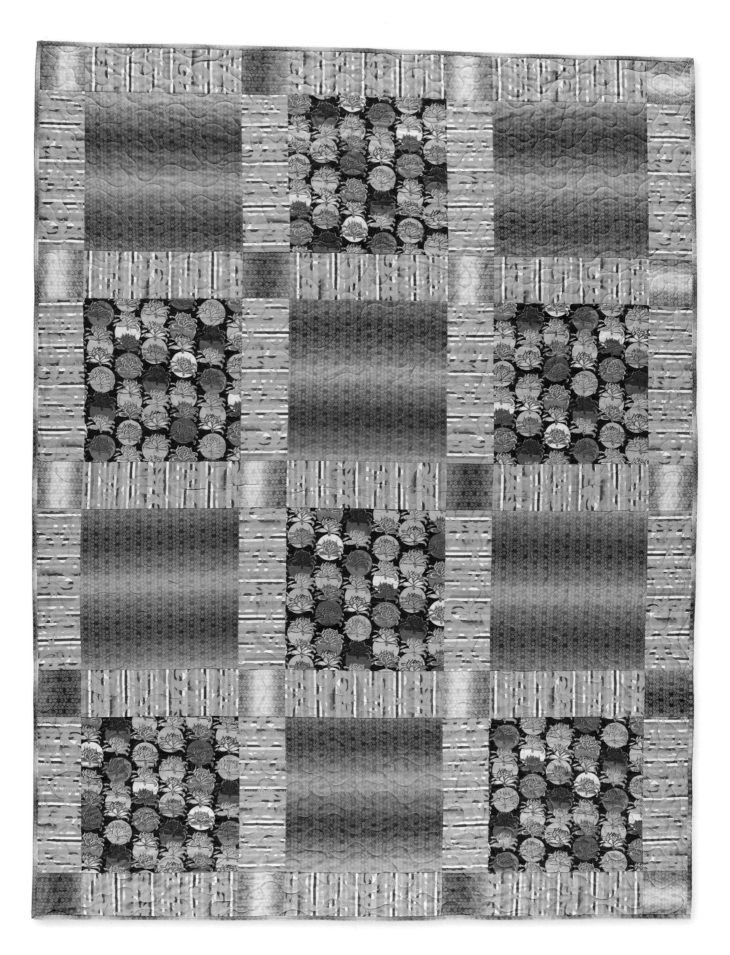

# color option

Customize "Spice It Up" and make it for a special youngster by "fussy cutting" a juvenile or novelty print for the large squares. To do it, select a specific part of a fabric print, such as the whimsical duck scenes on the print used here, and cut around it to the necessary cut size. This 61"-square quilt features nine fussy-cut blocks, surrounded with a multicolor stripe, and sashing squares and binding in a dimpled blue print.

## assemble quilt top

[1] Referring to **Quilt Assembly Diagram**, lay out the six orange floral squares, six mottled orange squares, 20 mottled green sashing squares, and 31 orange stripe sashing rectangles in nine horizontal rows.

[2] Sew together pieces in each row. Press seams toward sashing rectangles. Join rows to complete quilt top. Press seams in one direction.

## finish quilt

[1] Layer quilt top, batting, and backing; baste. (For details, see Quilt It, *page 197*.)

[2] Quilt as desired. This quilt was stitched with an allover large stipple pattern across the quilt top.

[3] Bind with mottled teal blue binding strips. (For details, see Better Binding, *page 206*.)

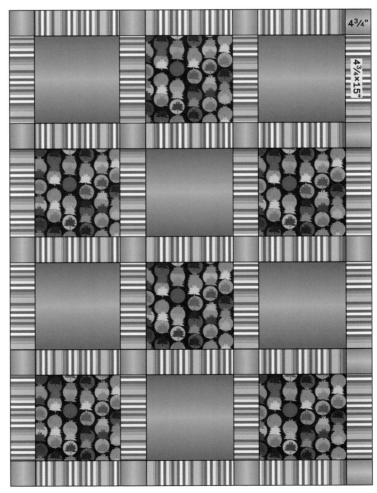

4³⁄₄"

4³⁄₄x15"

**QUILT ASSEMBLY DIAGRAM**

DESIGNER **CATH DERKSEMA AND KRISTEN JUNOR FOR PRINTS CHARMING**
PHOTOGRAPHS **GREG SCHEIDEMANN**

Three bright
prints make up
the merriest
Four-Patch
quilt around.

# four square

*Three bright starburst prints give a fresh twist to a traditional Four-Patch block. A bright white tone-on-tone print is the perfect foil to the lively prints.*

## materials

- 1½ yards blue print (blocks, binding)
- ⅝ yard green print (blocks)
- ⅝ yard red print (blocks)
- 1¾ yards white tone-on-tone (blocks, sashing, border)
- 3¼ yards backing fabric
- 57×65" batting

**Finished quilt:** 50½×59"
**Finished block:** 7½×8½"

**Quantities** are for 44/45"-wide, 100% cotton fabrics.
**Measurements** include ¼" seam allowances. Sew with right sides together unless otherwise stated.

tip    To avoid damage to your sewing machine and injury to yourself, don't sew over pins. Remove each pin just before the machine needle gets to it.

## cut fabrics

Cut pieces in the following order. Cut sashing and border strips lengthwise (parallel to selvage).

**From blue print, cut:**
- 6—2½×42" binding strips
- 60—4¼" squares

**From green print, cut:**
- 30—4¼" squares

**From red print, cut:**
- 30—4¼" squares

**From white tone-on-tone, cut:**
- 2—4¼×59" border strips
- 2—4¼×43" border strips
- 6—1½×43" sashing strips
- 25—1½×8" strips
- 10—1½×4¼" strips

## assemble blocks

[1] Referring to **Diagram 1**, sew together one blue print square and one red print square. Press seam in one direction. Repeat to join one green print square and one blue print square.

[2] Join one white tone-on-tone 1½×8" strip to Step 1 blue-red unit (**Diagram 2**). Join green-blue Step 1 unit to opposite edge of strip to make a block (**Diagram 3**). Press all seams toward squares. The block should be 8×9" including seam allowances.

[3] Repeat steps 1 and 2 to make 25 blocks total.

## assemble half blocks

[1] Referring to **Diagram 4**, lay out one red print square, one white tone-on-tone 1½×4¼" strip, and one blue print square. Sew together pieces to make a pieced half block. Press seams toward squares. The half block should be 4¼×9" including seam allowances.

[2] Repeat Step 1 to make five red half blocks.

[3] Referring to **Diagram 5**, sew together red half blocks in a row to make a pieced red half-block strip.

[4] Using remaining blue print squares, white tone-on-tone 1½×4¼" strips, and green print squares, repeat steps 1 through 3 to make a green half-block strip.

## assemble quilt center

[1] Referring to **Quilt Assembly Diagram**, lay out blocks, white tone-on-tone 1½×43" sashing strips, red half-block strip, and green half-block strip in 13 horizontal rows.

[2] Sew together blocks in each block row. Press seams in one direction. Join rows to make quilt center; press seams in one direction.The quilt center should be 43×51½" including seam allowances.

## add border

Join white tone-on-tone 4¼×43" border strips to short edges of quilt center. Sew white tone-on-tone 4¼×59" border strips to remaining edges to complete quilt top. Press all seams toward border.

## finish quilt

[1] Layer quilt top, batting, and backing; baste. (For details, see Quilt It, *page 197*.)

[2] Quilt as desired. This quilt was machine-quilted with spiraling circles at the center of each multicolored Four-Patch, smaller spiraling circles in the half blocks, and a meandering loop pattern in the sashing and borders.

[3] Bind with blue print binding strips. (For details, see Better Binding, *page 206*.)

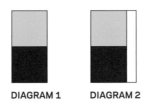

DIAGRAM 1    DIAGRAM 2

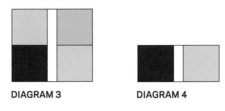

DIAGRAM 3    DIAGRAM 4

DIAGRAM 5

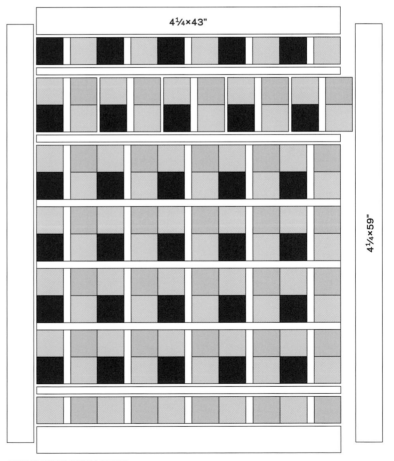

4¼×43"

4¼×59"

**QUILT ASSEMBLY DIAGRAM**

# hourglass pillow

Four triangles make a merry, square pillow! Three bright prints form the hourglass block pillow. Complete it with a covered button center and piped edging.

## materials

- ⅝ yard blue print
- ⅝ yard red print
- ⅝ yard green print
- 18"-square pillow form
- 2¼ yards ³⁄₁₆"-wide cotton cording
- 2—1⅛"-diameter cover buttons
- Doll maker's needle

Finished pillow: 18" square

**Quantities** are for 44/45"-wide, 100% cotton fabrics. **Measurements** include ¼" seam allowances. Sew with right sides together unless otherwise stated.

## cut fabrics

Cut pieces in the following order.

**From blue print, cut:**
- 1—19¼" square, cutting it diagonally twice in an X for 4 triangles total

**From red print, cut:**
- 1—19¼" square, cutting it diagonally twice in an X for 4 triangles total (you will use 2)
- 1—14" square, cutting it into enough 2¼"-wide strips to total 86" in length

**From green print, cut:**
- 1—19¼" square, cutting it diagonally twice in an X for 4 triangles total (you will use 2)

## assemble pillow (front and back)

[1] Sew together one red triangle and one blue triangle along one short edge to make a large red triangle unit (**Diagram 1**). Press seam toward red triangle.

[2] Join one green triangle and one blue triangle along one short edge to make a large green triangle unit (**Diagram 2**). Press seam toward green triangle.

**DIAGRAM 3**

[3] Sew together red and green triangle units to make pillow top. The pillow front should be 18½" square including seam allowances.

[4] Repeat steps 2 through 3 to make pillow back.

## finish pillow

[1] Cut and piece red print 2¼"-wide bias strips to make an 86"-long strip.

[2] Fold one strip end under 1½". With wrong side inside, fold strip in half lengthwise. Insert cording next to folded edge with cording end 1" from strip's folded end. Using a zipper foot, baste through fabric layers right next to cording to make piping (**Diagram 3**). Seam allowance should be ¼" wide.

[3] Aligning raw edges, baste piping to all edges of pillow front, starting 1½" from piping folded end. As you stitch each corner, clip seam allowance to within a few threads of stitching line (**Diagram 4**); gently ease piping in place. Cut end of cording to fit snugly inside folded opening, then stitch to beginning point to complete pillow top.

[4] Join pillow back to pillow top, stitching around all edges and leaving an opening for turning. Turn right side out, insert pillow form, and stitch opening closed.

[5] Following manufacturer's instructions, cover buttons with green print.

[6] Thread doll maker's needle with sturdy thread. Stitch down through center of pillow top, leaving a knot on top of pillow. Center one button on pillow back and one on pillow top. Taking long stitches through the center of pillow, sew buttons firmly in place.

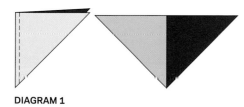

**DIAGRAM 1**

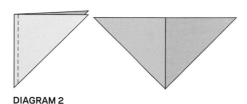

**DIAGRAM 2**

**DIAGRAM 4**

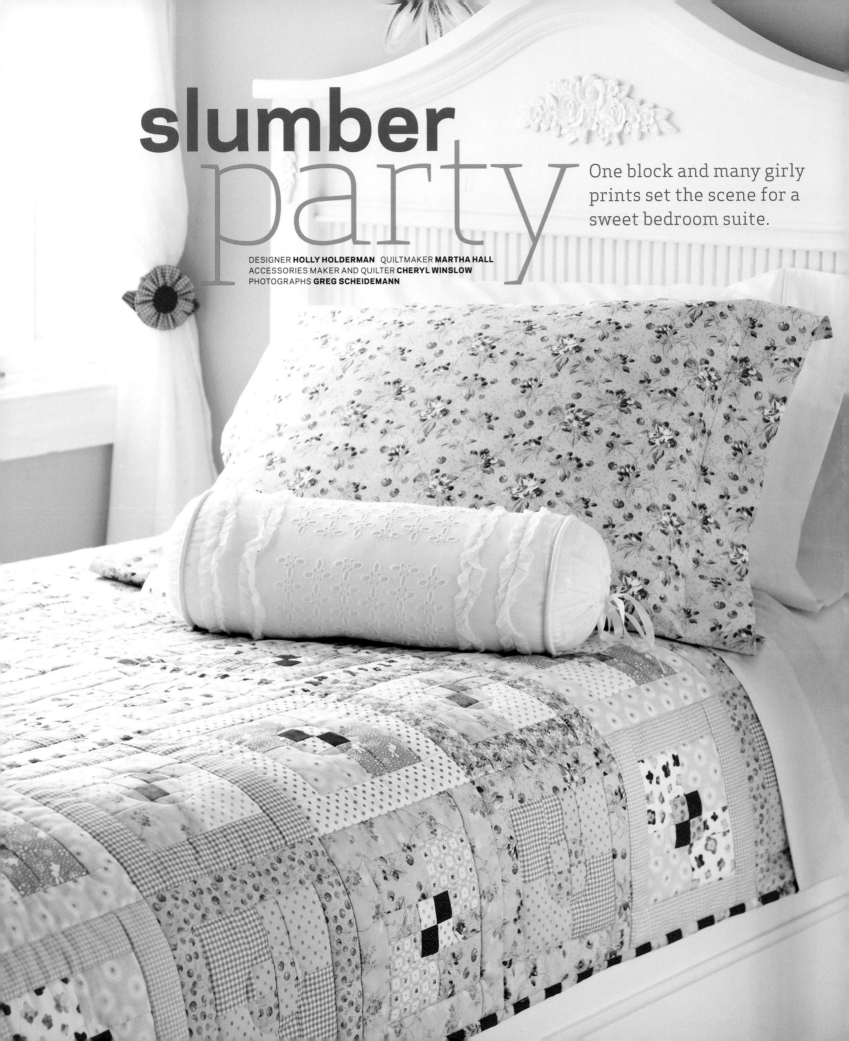

# slumber party

One block and many girly prints set the scene for a sweet bedroom suite.

DESIGNER **HOLLY HOLDERMAN**   QUILTMAKER **MARTHA HALL**
ACCESSORIES MAKER AND QUILTER **CHERYL WINSLOW**
PHOTOGRAPHS **GREG SCHEIDEMANN**

*What little girl wouldn't be all smiles with this delightful bedroom ensemble? Use a collection of 19 florals, checks, and polka-dot prints to create a bevy of blocks for the quilt and finish the room's dressings by making a coordinating flower tie back for the curtain.*

## for the quilt

## materials

- 2 yards total assorted pink prints (blocks, binding)
- 2⅝ yards total assorted green prints (blocks)
- 2 yards total assorted light pink prints (blocks)
- ¾ yard dark pink print (blocks, binding)
- ⅛ yard dark green print (blocks)
- ⅜ yard total assorted light green prints (blocks)
- 1 yard white-and-pink flower print (blocks)
- 6 yards backing fabric
- 70×106" batting

Finished quilt: 63½×99½"
Finished block: 9" square

Quantities are for 44/45"-wide, 100% cotton fabrics. Measurements include ¼" seam allowances. Sew with right sides together unless otherwise stated.

## cut fabrics

To replicate the look of the featured quilt, pieces are cut in matching sets. Use pins or clear sandwich bags to keep pieces and sets organized for assembly. See "Planning a Scrappy Quilt" on *page 37* for more specific details about color placement.

Cut pieces in the following order.

**From assorted pink prints, cut:**
- 12—1½×42" strips for binding
- 40—2×9½" rectangles (20 sets of two matching pieces)
- 40—2×6½" rectangles (20 sets of two matching pieces in same print as above)
- 98—2½×3½" rectangles (49 sets of two matching pieces)
- 98—1½×2½" rectangles (49 sets of two matching pieces in same print as above)
- 76—1½" squares (38 sets of two matching pieces)

**From assorted green prints, cut:**
- 68—2×9½" rectangles (34 sets of two matching pieces)
- 68—2×6½" rectangles (34 sets of two matching pieces in same print as above)
- 96—2½×3½" rectangles (48 sets of two matching pieces)
- 96—1½×2½" rectangles (48 sets of two matching pieces in same print as above)
- 92—1½" squares (46 sets of two matching pieces)

**From assorted light pink prints, cut:**
- 30—2×9½" rectangles (15 sets of two matching pieces)
- 30—2×6½" rectangles (15 sets of two matching pieces in same print as above)
- 78—2½×3½" rectangles (39 sets of two matching pieces)
- 78—1½×2½" rectangles (39 sets of two matching pieces in same print as above)
- 46—1½" squares (23 sets of two matching pieces)

**From dark pink print, cut:**
- 12—1½×42" strips for binding
- 62—1½" squares (31 sets of two)

**From dark green print, cut:**
- 32—1½" squares (16 sets of two)

**From assorted light green prints, cut:**
- 32—2½×3½" rectangles (16 sets of two matching pieces)
- 32—1½×2½" rectangles (16 sets of two matching pieces in same print as above)

**From white-and-pink flower print, cut:**
- 16—2×9½" rectangles (8 sets of two)
- 16—2×6½" rectangles (8 sets of two)
- 36—2½×3½" rectangles (18 sets of two)
- 36—1½×2½" rectangles (18 sets of two)

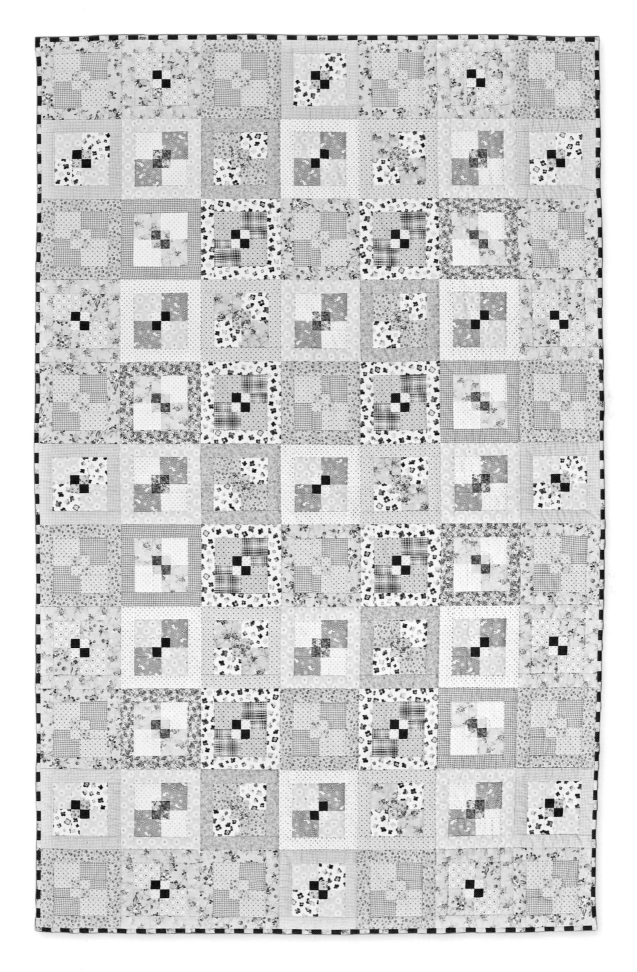

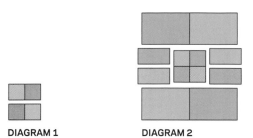

DIAGRAM 1

DIAGRAM 2

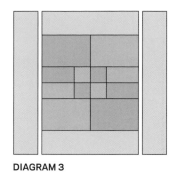

DIAGRAM 3

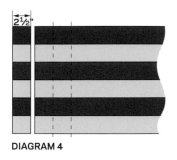

2½"

DIAGRAM 4

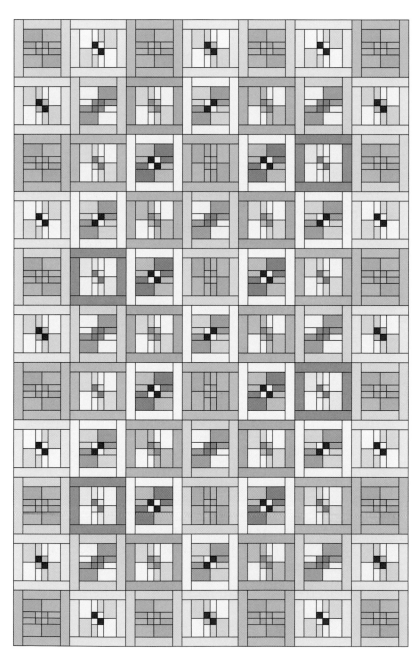

QUILT ASSEMBLY DIAGRAM

## assemble four-patch units

[1] Referring to **Diagram 1**, sew together two matching pink print 1½" squares and two matching green print 1½" squares in pairs. Press seams in opposite directions. Join pairs to make a pink/green Four-Patch unit. Press seam in one direction. The unit should be 2½" square including seam allowances.

[2] Repeat Step 1 to make 30 pink/green Four-Patch units total.

[3] Using matching light pink print and matching dark pink print squares, repeat Step 1 to make 23 light pink/dark pink Four-Patch units.

[4] Using matching pink print and matching dark pink print squares, repeat Step 1 to make eight pink/dark pink Four-Patch units.

[5] Using matching green print and matching dark green print squares, repeat Step 1 to make 16 green/dark green Four-Patch units.

## assemble blocks

For each block, you'll need a Four-Patch unit and three more sets of matching fabric pieces. When making blocks, make them as scrappy or as planned as you like. (See "Planning a Scrappy Quilt" to read about designer Holly Holderman's design that looks scrappy, but is actually very carefully planned.)

[1] To make a block, you'll need one Four-Patch unit; two 2½×3½" rectangles and two 1½×2½" rectangles from one print; two 2½×3½" rectangles and two 1½×2½" rectangles from a second print; and two 2×9½" rectangles and two 2×6½" rectangles from a third print.

[2] Referring to **Diagram 2**, lay out Four-Patch unit and the first two sets of pieces in rows. Join print 1½×2½" rectangles on either side of Four-Patch unit. Press seams toward darker print. Then sew together pieces in each row. Press seams in one direction, alternating direction with each row. Join rows to make a block unit. Press seams in one direction. The unit should be 6½" square including seam allowances.

[3] Sew print 2×6½" rectangles to opposite edges of block unit. Add print 2×9½" rectangles to remaining edges to make a block (**Diagram 3**). Press all seams toward rectangles. The block should be 9½" square including seam allowances.

[4] Repeat steps 1 through 3 to make 77 blocks total.

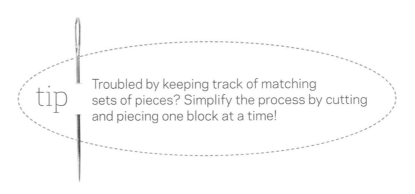

**tip**  Troubled by keeping track of matching sets of pieces? Simplify the process by cutting and piecing one block at a time!

## assemble quilt top

[1] Referring to **Quilt Assembly Diagram**, lay out blocks in 11 horizontal rows.

[2] Sew together blocks in each row. Press seams in one direction, alternating direction with each row.

[3] Join rows to complete quilt top. Press seams in one direction.

## assemble pieced binding

[1] Alternating colors, sew together three dark pink print 1½×42" strips and three assorted pink print 1½×42" strips to make a strip set (**Diagram 4**). Press seams open to reduce bulk. Repeat to make four strip sets total. Cut strip sets into 56—2½"-wide segments total.

[2] Cut and piece enough 2½"-wide segments to make:
  ‣ 2—99½"-long binding strips
  ‣ 2—64½"-long binding strips

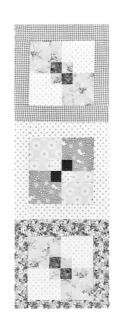

## planning a scrappy quilt

Designer Holly Holderman and quiltmaker Martha Hall made a quilt that looks scrappy but is really carefully planned. If you want to duplicate their look, pay attention to fabrics used in each block, combining the same pink print with the same green print in a series of blocks.

Make your blocks as scrappy or as planned as you like. For each block, you'll need to choose sets of matching pieces; for uniform blocks, use the same green print throughout, or for more variety, use three different green prints in one block.

## color option

To duplicate this one-for-the-boys variation of "Slumber Party," make 25 blocks using five assorted prints for each block. We made the 45"-square throw from a variety of fat quarter pieces from Strawberry Lemonade by Me & My Sister Designs for Moda, then assembled them in a casual, no-planning-required setting. It's easy to customize this pattern for any recipient. Jazz it up with brights and lights, or tone it down with neutrals or monochromatic fabrics.

QUILTMAKERS **JACALYN BELL AND LYNN MERTEN**
PHOTOGRAPH **MARTY BALDWIN**

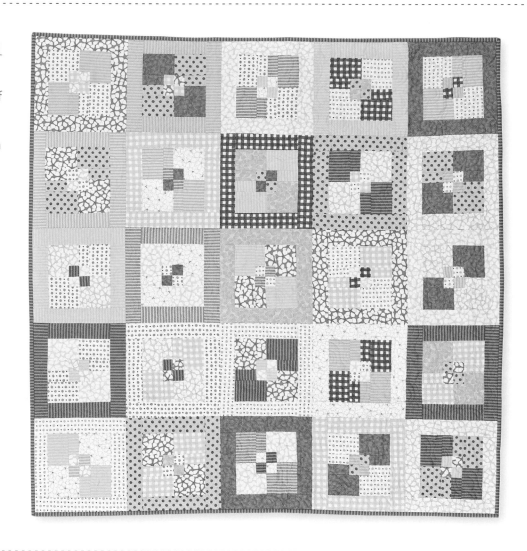

**Fold under ½".**

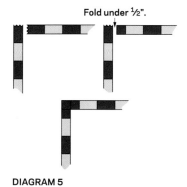

**DIAGRAM 5**

## finish quilt

[**1**] Layer quilt top, batting, and backing; baste. (For details, see Quilt It, *page 197*.)

[**2**] Quilt as desired. This quilt was stitched in the ditch between blocks and around each block center. A circle was quilted around the Four-Patch unit in the center of each block.

[**3**] Bind side edges of quilt top with long binding strips. Bind top and bottom edges with short binding strips, turning ends under ½" before stitching closed (**Diagram 5**). (For details, see Better Binding, *page 206*.)

## for one fabric flower

Whether you use them as a curtain tie-back, or stitch them to a pillow top, these flowers bring a cheerful finishing touch to your room ensemble.

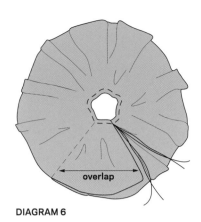

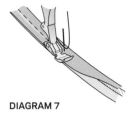

**DIAGRAM 6**

**DIAGRAM 7**

## materials

- ▸ 7" square green print (leaf)
- ▸ 1/8 yard pink print (flower)
- ▸ Scrap of pink check (covered button)
- ▸ 4¼" square green print (loop)
- ▸ 9" piece of ¼"-diameter piece of cotton cording

Finished flower: 4" diameter

## cut fabrics

Patterns can be found on *Pattern Sheet 2.* To make templates of patterns, see "What Are Templates?" on *page 201.*

**From green print, cut:**
- ▸ 2 of Leaf Pattern

**From pink print, cut:**
- ▸ 1—3½×23½" strip

**From pink felt, cut:**
- ▸ 1 of Circle Pattern

**From green print square, cut:**
- ▸ 1—1½×12" bias strip

## assemble flower

[1] Sew together leaf pieces, right sides together, with a scant ¼" seam, leaving an opening for turning in middle of one long edge. Clip across each leaf point, then turn right side out. Press the leaf then slip-stitch opening closed.

[2] Clip short ends of pink print 3½×23½" strip with pinking shears to prevent raveling. Fold short ends in ¼"; press. Fold strip in half lengthwise; press.

[3] Using a long stitch length, sew ⅛" from long raw edges of the folded strip. Pull thread to gather the strip into a tight circle. Overlap ends about 1" (**Diagram 6**) and tie thread ends in a knot to secure.

[4] Center pink felt circle piece over hole on flower back; slip-stitch to flower back (this secures the flower shape and provides a sturdy background upon which to sew the button).

[5] Following manufacturer's directions, cover button with scrap of pink check. Center button atop flower and leaf. Hand-stitch button in place through all layers to complete fabric flower.

[6] With the wrong side inside, fold under 1½" at one end of the bias strip. With wrong side inside, fold the strip in half lengthwise to make the cording cover. Insert the cording next to the folded edge, placing a cording end 1" from the cording cover folded end. Using a machine cording foot, sew through both fabric layers right next to the cording. Trim the excess fabric close to the seam (**Diagram 7**).

[7] Hand-stitch both ends of the covered cording to the center back of the rosette, forming a loop. Thread the loop of the completed rosette through a ribbon or fabric tie-back.

DESIGNERS **SARAH MAXWELL AND DOLORES SMITH**
PHOTOGRAPHS **GREG SCHEIDEMANN**

# puzzle
## play

It's a simple brick
assembly, but the
pinwheel-style
arrangement
gives it a whole
new spin.

*The trick to this double-bed-size pattern is in the way you set and sew the simple blocks together. Use a design wall or other flat surface to lay out the eight rectangles for each block in the quilt center, like building a brick patio (two horizontal rectangles adjoining two vertical rectangles). Assemble the blocks one at a time and replace on design wall. Then join the blocks in diagonal rows to make the quilt center. The block design continues into the outer border.*

## materials

- 5 yards total assorted blue prints (blocks, inner and outer borders)
- 5 yards total assorted red, yellow, green, and cream prints (blocks, outer border)
- ¾ yard blue polka dot (binding)
- 5½ yards backing fabric
- 82×99" batting

Finished quilt: 76×93"
Finished blocks: 10" square; 6½" square

Quantities are for 44/45"-wide, 100% cotton fabrics. Measurements include ¼" seam allowances. Sew with right sides together unless otherwise stated.

## cut fabrics

Cut pieces in the following order.

**From one blue print, cut:**
- 3—1⅞×42" strips for inner border
- 4—1¼×9¾" rectangles for outer border

**From assorted blue prints, cut:**
- 14—11" squares, cutting each diagonally twice in an X for 56 border setting triangles total
- 8—5½" squares, cutting each in half diagonally for 16 border corner triangles total
- 200—3×5½" rectangles (50 sets of 4 matching rectangles)

**From assorted red, yellow, and green prints, cut:**
- 128—2⅛×3¾" rectangles (32 sets of 4 matching rectangles)

**From assorted cream prints, cut:**
- 128—2⅛×3¾" rectangles (32 sets of 4 matching rectangles)

**From remaining assorted red, yellow, green, and cream prints, cut:**
- 200—3×5½" rectangles (50 sets of 4 matching rectangles)

**From blue polka dot, cut:**
- 9—2½×42" binding strips

## assemble blocks

For each block, you'll need four matching blue print rectangles and four assorted print rectangles. The assorted prints selected for each block will match up with identical fabrics in adjacent blocks to continue the design across the quilt top (**Quilt Assembly Diagram**). Use a design wall for layout.

[1] Aligning long edges, sew together a blue print 3×5½" rectangle and an assorted print 3×5½" rectangle to make a rectangle unit (**Diagram 1**). Press seam in one direction. Using matching blue print pieces, repeat to make four rectangle units total.

DIAGRAM 1          DIAGRAM 2

[2] Sew together rectangle units in pairs (**Diagram 2**). Press seams in opposite directions. Join pairs to make a block; press seam in one direction. The block should be 10½" square including seam allowances.

[3] Repeat steps 1 and 2 to make 50 blocks total.

**QUILT ASSEMBLY DIAGRAM**

## assemble quilt center

[1] Referring to **Quilt Assembly Diagram**, lay out blocks in diagonal rows. Sew together blocks in each row. Press seams in one direction, alternating direction with each row. Join rows to make quilt center; press seams in one direction.

[2] Trim quilt center edges ¼" from centers of outer blocks (**Diagram 3**). The quilt center should be 57½×71¾" including seam allowances.

## add inner border

[1] Cut and piece blue print 1⅞×42" strips to make:
  ‣ 2—1⅞×57½" inner border strips

[2] Sew inner border strips to short edges of quilt center. Press seams toward inner border.

tip

Use the flannel back of a vinyl tablecloth for a design wall, rolling it up between projects or hanging one in front of the other to view different quilt projects.

## assemble and add outer border

[1] Referring to Assemble Blocks, *page 41*, steps 1 and 2, use four matching cream print 2⅛×3¾" rectangles and four matching red, yellow, or green print 2⅛×3¾" rectangles to make a border block (**Diagram 4**). The border block should be 7" square including seam allowances. Repeat to make 32 border blocks total.

[2] Referring to **Diagram 5**, sew border setting triangles to opposite edges of a border block to make unit A. Triangle points will extend past adjacent edges of block. Press seams toward setting triangles. Repeat to make 24 total of unit A.

[3] Join a border setting triangle and a border corner triangle to opposite edges of a border block (**Diagram 6**). Center and add a border corner triangle to one remaining edge to make unit B. Press all seams toward triangles. Repeat to make eight total of unit B.

**DIAGRAM 3**

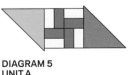

**DIAGRAM 4**

**DIAGRAM 5**
**UNIT A**

**DIAGRAM 6**
**UNIT B**

DIAGRAM 7

[4] Sew together six A units and two B units to make an outer border strip (**Diagram 7**). Press seams in one direction. The outer border strip should be 9¾×74½" including seam allowances. Repeat to make four outer border strips total.

[5] Sew outer border strips to long edges of quilt center (**Diagram 7**). Press seams toward outer border.

[6] Join a blue print 1¼×9¾" rectangle to each end of remaining outer border strips to make two pieced outer border strips (**Diagram 7**). Press seams toward rectangles. Sew pieced outer border strips to remaining edges to complete quilt top.

## finish quilt

[1] Layer quilt top, batting, and backing; baste. (For details, see Quilt It, *page 197*.)

[2] Quilt as desired. This quilt features an allover swirl design stitched in the quilt center. For the outer border, a floral motif is quilted in each setting triangle and a curl design is in each block.

[3] Bind with blue polka dot binding strips. (For details, see Better Binding, *page 206*.)

QUILTMAKER **JUDY SOHN**
PHOTOGRAPHS **GREG SCHEIDEMANN**

# square off

Mix it up!
Colorful stripes with prints
of all sizes come together in
a quick-to-make throw.

*What's the secret for making this cozy
quilt? A quick stitch-and-flip method
of adding corners to 8" squares.
Select assorted prints and polka dots
for the squares and pair each with a
complementary stripe. Design as you
go—just stitch the blocks and lay them
out to suit your fancy.*

## materials

- ⅝ yard each green, blue, and red stripes (blocks)
- 3½ yards total assorted yellow, red, orange, green, blue, and tan prints and polka dots (blocks)
- ⅝ yard blue print (binding)
- 3¾ yards backing fabric
- 67" square batting

Finished quilt: 60½" square
Finished block: 7½" square

Quantities are for 44/45"-wide,
100% cotton fabrics.
Measurements include ¼" seam
allowances. Sew with right sides
together unless otherwise stated.

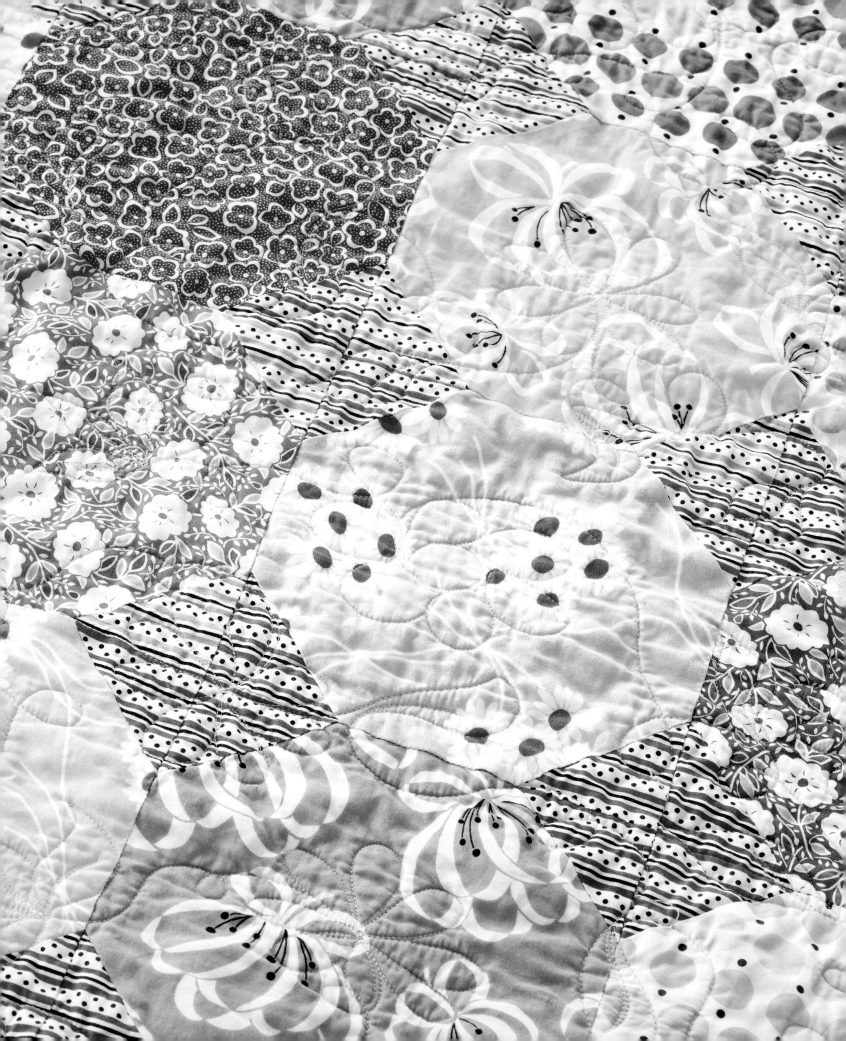

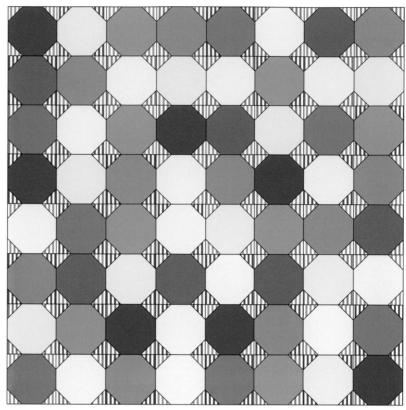

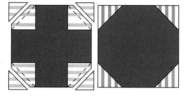

**BLOCK ASSEMBLY DIAGRAM**

**QUILT ASSEMBLY DIAGRAM**

## cut fabrics

Cut pieces in the following order.

**From green, blue, and red stripes, cut:**
▸ 256—2¾" squares (64 sets of 4 matching squares)

**From assorted yellow, red, orange, green, blue, and tan prints and polka dots, cut:**
▸ 64—8" squares

**From blue print, cut:**
▸ 7—2½×42" binding strips

## assemble blocks

[1] Use a pencil to mark a diagonal line on wrong side of each green, blue, and red stripe 2¾" square. See Editor's Tip opposite for help with marking squares. (To prevent fabric from tretching as you draw the lines, place 220-grit sandpaper under each square.)

[2] Align a marked green, blue, or red stripe 2¾" square with one corner of an assorted print or polka dot 8" square (**Block Assembly Diagram**; note direction of marked line). Sew on drawn line; trim excess fabric, leaving ¼" seam allowance. Press open attached triangle.

[3] Repeat Step 2 to add three marked matching 2¾" squares to remaining corners of print or polka dot 8" square to make a block (**Block Assembly Diagram**; again note direction of drawn lines). The block should be 8" square including seam allowances.

[4] Repeat steps 2 and 3 to make 64 blocks total.

## assemble quilt center

[1] Referring to **Quilt Assembly Diagram** for placement, lay out blocks in eight rows.

[2] Sew together blocks in each row. Press seams in one direction, alternating direction with each row. Join rows to make quilt top. Press seams in one direction.

## finish quilt

[1] Layer quilt top, batting, and backing; baste. (For details, see Quilt It, *page 197*.)

[2] Quilt as desired. This quilt features an allover floral and loop pattern.

[3] Bind with blue print binding strips. (For details, see Better Binding, *page 206*.)

tip

Change direction as you mark lines on each set of matching stripe squares. With stripes running in the same direction, mark two squares with diagonal lines from top left corner to bottom right and two squares from bottom left corner to top right.

# color option

Using a stash of flannels, this version of "Square Off" has a warm and cozy look. Make yours as scrappy as you like. We chose six ⅞-yard pieces in a soft palette of yellow, green, blue, periwinkle, and cloud white.

For blocks that will stand out in a subtle color scheme, alternate placement of light and dark blocks.

**tip** Changing the number of colors used can dramatically change the finished look of a quilt pattern. To experiment, use colored pencils and graph paper to first sketch a design.

DESIGNER **KAREN MONTGOMERY**
PHOTOGRAPHS **GREG SCHEIDEMANN**

# around
## the block

Learn a quick way to construct mitered blocks from stripe fabric.
Alternate mitered blocks with printed squares for a fast finish.

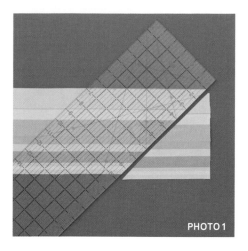

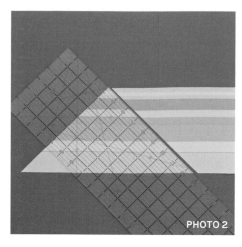

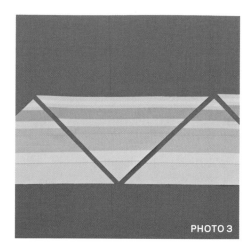

*The secret to these mitered blocks lies in accurately cutting the triangles. First you rotary-cut alternating triangles from sections of the stripe fabric, then you simply piece the bias edges together. Using the walking foot attachment on your sewing machine keeps the edges from stretching.*

## materials

- 1⅝ yards pastel stripe running lengthwise (parallel to the selvages) (blocks)
- ⅓ yard each blue, coral, and tan prints; blue leaf; tan floral; and solid green (setting squares)
- ⅔ yard solid light blue (binding)
- 4¼ yards backing fabric
- 73" square batting
- Spray sizing or starch
- 12"-square acrylic ruler

Finished quilt: 67" square
Finished block: 9½" square

Quantities are for 44/45"-wide, 100% cotton fabrics. Measurements include ¼" seam allowances. Sew with right sides together unless otherwise stated.

## cut fabrics

Cut pieces in the following order. Cut pastel stripe strips lengthwise (parallel to the selvages).

**From pastel stripe, cut:**
- 7—6×54" strips

**From each blue, coral, and tan print; blue leaf; tan floral; and solid green, cut:**
- 4—10" setting squares

**From solid light blue, cut:**
- 7—2½×42" binding strips

## assemble blocks

[1] Place an acrylic ruler on one pastel stripe 6×54" strip, aligning 45° line along bottom edge of fabric (**Photo 1**). Cut along right edge of ruler.

[2] Rotate cutting mat, leaving strip in same position. Place right-hand edge of ruler at top corner of first cut and align a cross line on ruler with first cut edge (**Photo 2**); cut along right edge to make one triangle.

[3] Continue rotating cutting mat and alternating ruler position to cut 16 triangles total from each strip (**Photo 3**). Group identical triangles in sets of four. Note: The short sides of each triangle are bias edges; handle them carefully to avoid distortion.

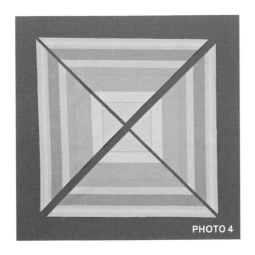

PHOTO 4

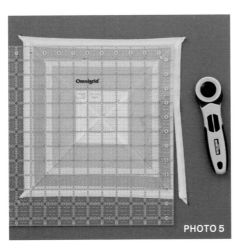

PHOTO 5

[4] Lay out an identical triangle set in pairs (**Photo 4**). Sew together triangles in each pair, carefully matching stripes. Press seams in opposite directions. (If the triangle pairs don't align evenly, see "Making the Halves Match," *page 54*.) Join pairs to make a block, matching center seams and stripes. Press seam in one direction. The block should be 11½" square including seam allowances. Repeat to make 25 blocks total. (You will have three triangle sets left over.)

[5] Referring to **Photo 5**, place 12½"-square acrylic ruler on a block, aligning intersection of 5" lines with block center. Trim block along edges of ruler. Reposition ruler and trim opposite side of block in same manner. The block should now be 10" square including seam allowances. Repeat to trim each block.

## assemble quilt top

Referring to **Quilt Assembly Diagram** for placement, lay out blocks and setting squares in seven rows. Sew together pieces in each row; press seams toward setting squares. Join rows to make quilt top. Press seams in one direction.

## finish quilt

[1] Layer quilt top, batting, and backing; baste. (For details, see Quilt It, *page 197*.)

[2] Quilt as desired. The blocks in the featured quilt are stitched along edges of stripes, giving the appearance of in-the-ditch quilting. Each setting square is quilted with three concentric rectangles.

[3] Bind with solid light blue binding strips. (For details, see Better Binding, *page 206*.)

**QUILT ASSEMBLY DIAGRAM**

# making the halves match

The key to precisely matched stripes is joining identical halves. For this project, pieces are cut larger than necessary to allow for trimming. If the triangle pairs for one block are distorted, trim each pair before stitching them together.

Place an acrylic ruler on the distorted triangle pair, aligning a cross line on the ruler with the seam; trim (**Photo A**).

Measure the distance from the ruler's edge to one stripe on the fabric. For the remaining triangle pair, measure the same distance from the same stripe; trim to make an identical half (**Photo B**).

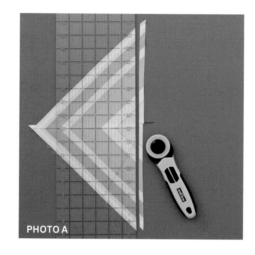

PHOTO A

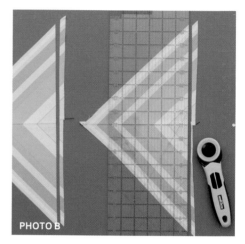

PHOTO B

**tip** Use a generous amount of spray sizing on the stripe fabric before cutting—this will help stabilize the bias edges as you assemble the blocks.

# red-&-white delight

Make a simple two-color quilt and matching pillowcases with an unexpected combination of reverse-color prints.

DESIGNER **MABETH OXENREIDER**
PHOTOGRAPHS **ADAM ALBRIGHT**

*Even though this quilt is easily made of squares with sashing and a border, it's bound to be a classic. Select a single, main color and add a white coordinating print, such as the red and white fabrics used on this quilt. White-and-red bands bring the red pillowcases to life, providing bold accents for the queen-size quilt.*

## for the quilt

### materials

- 4⅛ yards red print (squares, binding)
- 6⅞ yards white-and-red print* (sashing, border)
- 8 yards backing fabric
- 96×115" batting

*See Cut Fabrics.

Finished quilt: 90×109"

Quantities are for 44/45"-wide, 100% cotton fabrics. Measurements include ¼" seam allowances. Sew with right sides together unless otherwise stated.

## cut fabrics

Cut pieces in the following order. Cut sashing and border strips lengthwise (parallel to the selvages) where indicated. The yardage given for border and sashing strips allows for the most economical use of fabric. If you prefer to cut all strips lengthwise, you will need 8¼ yards of white-and-red print.

**From red print, cut:**
- 17—6×42" strips
- 11—2½×42" binding strips

**From white-and-red print, cut:**
- 2—4½×109" border strips (lengthwise)
- 8—4½×101" sashing strips (lengthwise)
- 2—4½×82" border strips (lengthwise)
- 16—4½×42" strips (cut 12 lengthwise and 4 crosswise)

## assemble strip sets

[1] Join two red print 6×42" strips and one white-and-red print 4½×42" strip to make strip set A (**Strip Set A Diagram**). Press seams toward red print strips. Repeat to make six A strip sets total.

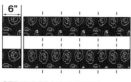

**STRIP SET A DIAGRAM**

[2] Cut A strip sets into 6"-wide segments to make 36 A units total.

[3] Join two white-and-red print 4½×42" strips and one red print 6×42" strip to make strip set B (**Strip Set B Diagram**). Press seams

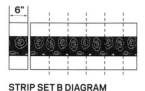

**STRIP SET B DIAGRAM**

toward red print strip. Repeat to make five B strip sets total.

[4] Cut B strip sets into 6"-wide segments to make 27 B units total.

## assemble quilt center

[1] Referring to **Quilt Assembly Diagram**, sew together four A units and three B units to make a pieced strip. Press seams toward A units. The pieced strip should be 6×101" including seam allowances. Repeat to make nine pieced strips total.

[2] Lay out pieced strips and white-and-red print sashing strips in rows (**Quilt Assembly Diagram**).

[3] Join rows to make quilt center. Press seams toward pieced strips. The quilt center should be 82×101" including seam allowances.

## for two pillowcases materials

▸ ⅝ yard white-and-red print (bands)
▸ 1⅔ yards red print (cases)

Finished Standard-Size Pillowcase: 20½×32½"

Quantities are for 44/45"-wide, 100% cotton fabrics. Measurements include ¼" seam allowances. Sew with right sides together unless otherwise stated.

## cut fabrics

**From white-and-red print, cut:**
▸ 2—8½×42" rectangles
**From red print, cut:**
▸ 2—42×29" rectangles

## add border

Sew short white-and-red print border strips to short edges of quilt center. Sew long white-and-red print border strips to remaining edges to complete quilt top. Press seams toward quilt center.

## finish quilt

[**1**] Layer quilt top, batting, and backing; baste. (For details, see Quilt It, *page 197*.)

[**2**] Quilt as desired. This quilt has a meandering stipple pattern stitched across the quilt top.

[**3**] Bind with red print binding strips. (For details, see Better Binding, *page 206*.)

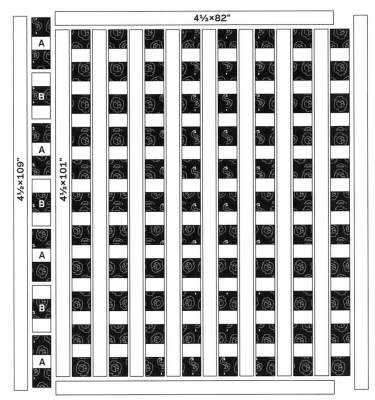

**QUILT ASSEMBLY DIAGRAM**

(diagram labels: 4½×82", 4½×109", 4½×101", A, B, A, B, A, B, A)

## assemble pillowcases

[**1**] Join short ends of a white-and-red print rectangle to form a circle.

[**2**] With wrong side inside, fold circle in half lengthwise to make a band; press.

[**3**] Fold red print rectangle in half crosswise to make a 21×29" rectangle. Sew together long edges and edges of one short end to make a case. Turn right side out; press.

[**4**] Matching raw edges, slide folded band around open end of case; pin (**Diagram 1**). Join pieces, stitching through all layers to make a pillowcase. Turn band right side out; press seam toward case. Topstitch along case edge near band (**Diagram 2**).

[**5**] Repeat steps 1–4 to make second pillowcase.

**DIAGRAM 1**

**DIAGRAM 2**

62

87

84

69

# in the kitchen

Whip up a fun project for the most used room in the house—the kitchen. Place mats, table runners, coasters, aprons, and even a reusable market bag will satisfy your quilting cravings.

Serve It Up ........................................ 62
To Market, To Market ..................... 66
Flower Market ................................... 69
Apron Strings ................................... 74
All About Stripes ............................. 81
Top This ............................................ 84
Everyday Elegance ......................... 87

# serve it up

Zigzag-stitch fusible words and motifs onto bright place mats to delight your guests with or without the dinnerware.

DESIGNER **LINDA LUM DEBONO**
PHOTOGRAPHS **GREG SCHEIDEMANN**

*This cheerful project is easily finished in a day. Just pick some colorful fat quarters from your stash and add a few complementary fabrics for a great gift or accent to your home. To liven up a holiday table, choose festive words and fabrics in seasonal colors.*

## materials

- Appliqué thread to match or contrast
- Lightweight fusible web
- Tear-away stabilizer

**Chat Place Mat**
- 9×22" piece (fat eighth) each of mottled pink, pink-and-white print, and bright pink print
- 6×12" piece each of mottled dark brown and mottled bright pink
- Scrap of pink-and-orange print
- 18×22" piece (fat quarter) pink floral
- 18×22" piece (fat quarter) backing fabric
- ⅜ yard quilt or craft batting

**Drink Place Mat**
- 9×22" piece (fat eighth) each of mottled pink, bright pink print, and pink-and-orange print
- 6×12" piece mottled dark brown
- 4×6" piece solid yellow-green
- Scrap of bright green print
- 18×22" piece (fat quarter) pink floral
- 18×22" piece (fat quarter) backing fabric
- ⅜ yard quilt or craft batting

**Enjoy Place Mat**
- 9×22" piece (fat eighth) each of blue, green, and blue-and-green prints
- 6×12" piece mottled dark brown

- 18×22" piece (fat quarter) green-and-turquoise floral
- 18×22" piece (fat quarter) backing fabric
- ⅜ yard quilt or craft batting

Finished place mats: 19×13"

Quantities are for 44/45"-wide, 100% cotton fabrics. Measurements include a ¼" seam allowance. Sew with right sides together unless otherwise stated.

**DIAGRAM 1**

**DIAGRAM 2**

**DIAGRAM 3**

## general instructions

When making place mats, refer to specific place mat instructions and the photographs opposite and on *page 63*. Patterns can be found on *Pattern Sheet 1*. To use fusible web for appliquéing, complete the following steps.

[1] Lay fusible web, paper side up, over patterns. Use a pencil to trace patterns the number of times indicated in specific place mat cutting instructions, leaving at least ½" between tracings. Cut out fusible-web shapes roughly ¼" outside traced lines.

[2] Following manufacturer's instructions, press fusible-web shapes onto backs of designated fabrics; let cool. Cut out fabric shapes on drawn lines and peel off paper backings.

## cut and assemble "chat" place mat

**From mottled pink, cut:**
‣ 1—11½x5½" rectangle for appliqué foundation
**From pink-and-white print, cut:**
‣ 2—8½x5½" rectangles for appliqué foundations
**From bright pink print, cut:**
‣ 1—8½x3½" rectangle
**From mottled dark brown, cut:**
‣ 1 each of letters C, H, A, and T
**From mottled bright pink, cut:**
‣ 2 of Pattern A
**From pink-and-orange print, cut:**
‣ 2 of Pattern B
**From pink floral, cut:**
‣ 1—11½x8½" rectangle
**From backing fabric, cut:**
‣ 1—19½x13½" rectangle
**From batting, cut:**
‣ 1—19½x13½" rectangle

[1] Referring to **Diagram 1**, lay out mottled dark brown letters on mottled pink rectangle and A flowers and B flower centers on pink-and-white print rectangles; fuse in place.

[2] Using thread to match the appliqués, machine-zigzag-stitch around each piece. (To avoid puckers, designer Linda Lum DeBono recommends placing stabilizer behind the appliqué foundations; remove it after stitching around appliqués.)

[3] Referring to **Diagram 1**, join appliquéd rectangles, bright pink print rectangle, and pink floral rectangle in two vertical rows. Press seams in one direction. Join rows to make place mat top. Press seam in one direction.

[4] Baste batting rectangle to wrong side of place mat top, machine-stitching a scant ¼" from the edges. Trim batting close to the scant ¼" seam, especially around the corners. With right sides together, layer the place mat and backing rectangle. Sew together, leaving a 4" opening along one side.

[5] Turn place mat and backing right side out through opening. Hand-stitch opening closed; press. Topstitch ¼" from place mat outer edges through all layers.

## cut and assemble "drink" place mat

**From mottled pink, cut:**
▸ 1—11×5½" rectangle for appliqué foundation

**From bright pink print, cut:**
▸ 1—6½×8½" rectangle for appliqué foundation
▸ 1 of Pattern E

**From pink-and-orange print, cut:**
▸ 1—9×5½" rectangle

**From mottled dark brown, cut:**
▸ 1 each of letters D, R, I, N, and K
▸ 1 of Pattern F

**From solid yellow-green, cut:**
▸ 1 of Pattern C

**From bright green print, cut:**
▸ 1 of Pattern D

**From pink floral, cut:**
▸ 1—13½×8½" rectangle

**From backing fabric, cut:**
▸ 1—19½×13½" rectangle

**From batting, cut:**
▸ 1—19½×13½" rectangle

[1] Referring to **Diagram 2**, lay out mottled dark brown letters on mottled pink rectangle and pieces C–F on bright pink print rectangle; fuse in place.

[2] Referring to Cut and Assemble "Chat" Place Mat, steps 2 through 5, assemble place mat.

## cut and assemble "enjoy" place mat

**From blue print, cut:**
▸ 1—11½×5½" rectangle for appliqué foundation

**From green print, cut:**
▸ 1—6½×8½" rectangle for appliqué foundation

**From blue-and-green print, cut:**
▸ 1—8½×5½" rectangle

**From mottled dark brown, cut:**
▸ 1 each of letters E, N, J, O, and Y
▸ 1 of Pattern G

**From green-and-turquoise floral, cut:**
▸ 1—13½×8½" rectangle

**From backing fabric, cut:**
▸ 1—19½×13½" rectangle

**From batting, cut:**
▸ 1—19½×13½" rectangle

[1] Referring to **Diagram 3**, lay out mottled dark brown letters on blue print rectangle and G mug on green print rectangle; fuse in place.

[2] Referring to Cut and Assemble "Chat" Place Mat, steps 2 through 5, assemble place mat.

# to market,
# to market

DESIGNER **MONICA SOLORIO-SNOW**
PHOTOGRAPHS **ADAM ALBRIGHT**

Keep multiples of this fun-to-make bag on hand for toting home farmer's market bounty or groceries.

*You'll never need to answer the question "Paper or plastic?" again. Make a few of these market bags, and not only are you an active part of the green movement— regardless of your bag's color—you're carrying your groceries in style.*

## materials

- ⅓ yard brown polka dot (casings)
- ¼ yard brown-and-yellow print (drawstring)
- ⅔ yard pink-and-brown print (bag)
- ⅔ yard muslin (lining)
- 2—½"-diameter buttons: white
- 2—1⅜"-wide novelty buttons: pink
- Large safety pin

Finished bag: 19×15×5"

Quantities are for 44/45"-wide, 100% cotton fabrics. Measurements include ¼" seam allowances. Sew with right sides together unless otherwise stated.

## cut fabrics

Cut pieces in the following order.

**From brown polka dot, cut:**
- 2—3½×39½" strips

**From brown-and-yellow print, cut:**
- 2—3×26¼" strips

**From pink-and-brown print, cut:**
- 2—20½" squares

**From muslin, cut:**
- 2—20½" squares

## assemble casings

[1] Fold a brown polka dot 3½×39½" strip in half widthwise and sew together across short ends to make a tube (**Diagram 1**). Press seam open.

[2] Turn tube to right side. Center seam and press tube flat. Fold tube in half lengthwise to make a 1¾×19½" casing (**Diagram 1**).

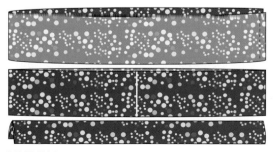

**DIAGRAM 1**

**DIAGRAM 2**

**DIAGRAM 3**

**DIAGRAM 4**

[3] Repeat steps 1 and 2 to make a second casing.

## assemble drawstring

[1] Join brown-and-yellow print 3×26¼" strips along short ends to make a 3×52" drawstring strip.

[2] Fold and lightly press drawstring strip in half lengthwise with wrong side inside. Open and press long edges to center. Refold in half and press. Topstitch ⅛" from outer edges to make drawstring (**Diagram 2**).

## assemble bag

[1] Center and pin raw edges of casing to one edge of pink-and-brown print 20½" square.

[2] Layer muslin 20½" lining square atop pink-and-brown square. Sew together top edges to make a bag unit (**Diagram 3**). Stitch top edges a second time to secure. Press seams toward brown-and-pink print.

[3] Repeat steps 1 and 2 to make a second bag unit. Press seams of second unit toward lining.

[4] Layer and pin bag units together. Sew together around all edges, leaving a 4" opening along bottom edge of lining for turning (**Diagram 4**). Trim corners. Press seams open.

[5] To shape flat bottom for bag, at one corner match bottom seam line to side seam line, creating a flattened triangle (**Diagram 5**).

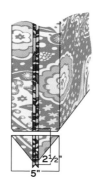

**DIAGRAM 5**

Measuring 2½" from point of triangle, draw a 5"-long line across triangle. Sew on drawn line. Trim excess fabric. Repeat with remaining bottom corner of bag and both corners of lining.

[6] Turn bag to right side and finger-press. Slip-stitch lining opening closed. Insert lining into bag.

[7] Using a large safety pin, thread drawstring through casings in a continuous loop. Overlap ends of drawstring by ¼". Sew ends together securely, stitching through overlapped layers.

[8] Center drawstring in casings so joined ends of drawstring rest in the middle of one casing. Tack drawstring in place, sewing through all layers. Layer and sew white and pink decorative buttons on top of tacking stitches. Tack remaining drawstring at center of opposite casing, adding decorative buttons as before.

DESIGNER **JUDY SOHN**
PHOTOGRAPHS **GREG SCHEIDEMANN**

# flower
## market

Quilt on the go! Pack this carry-along
project in your everyday tote.

No matter where your travels take you, you'll never have to leave home without a quilting project. You'll love the portability of traditional English paper piecing, a hand-sewing technique that involves stabilizing fabric with precut paper templates. Fill a zip-top bag with everything you need to make one of these tea-time coasters—fabric squares, paper hexagon templates, and needle and thread—and take off with project in hand.

- - - - - - - - - - - - - - - - - - - - - - - - - - - - - - - - - - - - -

## materials for one coaster

- 6×8" rectangle print No. 1 (flower)
- 18×24" rectangle print No. 2 (flower center, appliqué foundation, backing, binding)
- 9" square batting
- Precut ¾" hexagon paper

- templates or sturdy paper
- Hand-quilting thread

Finished coaster:
5½" diameter (3½" diameter patterns also included)

**tip** To make a smaller, 3½"-diameter coaster featuring ½" hexagons, use patterns C and D along with 2" fabric squares for the hexagons and 7" squares for the background and backing.

## cut fabrics

Cut pieces in the following order. Patterns can be found on *Pattern Sheet 2*. To make templates, use a pencil to trace Pattern A seven times and Pattern B once onto sturdy paper and cut out carefully and accurately.

**From print No. 1, cut:**
- 6—2½" squares

**From print No. 2, cut:**
- 2—9" squares
- 1—2½" square
- 1—1¾×18" bias binding strip (for details, see "Cutting on the Bias" on page 203)

## assemble hexagon appliqué

[1] To make hexagon appliqué using English paper piecing, pin a paper template to one print No. 1—2½" square. Cut around template, adding a ¼" seam allowance (**Photo 1**). The seam allowance does not have to be exact because the paper template will be an accurate guide. Repeat with remaining print No. 1 squares and print No. 2 square.

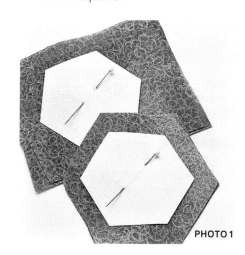

**PHOTO 1**

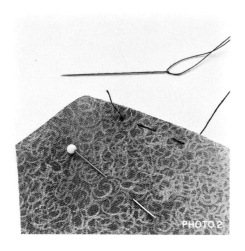

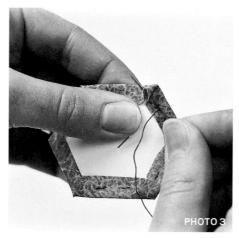

PHOTO 2

PHOTO 3

PHOTO 4

PHOTO 5

PHOTO 6

PHOTO 7

[2] Place template on wrong side of print No. 1 shape and fold seam allowance over one edge. Beginning with a knot on right side of fabric, baste seam allowance in place; stitch through fabric and paper template with ¼"-long basting stitches (**Photo 2**). Finger-press basted edge.

[3] As you approach a corner, fold seam allowance of next edge over template and continue stitching (**Photo 3**). Stitch all edges in same manner. Don't knot thread as you finish, and leave about a ½" thread tail on fabric's right side to make one print No. 1 hexagon piece. Do not remove paper template.

[4] Repeat steps 2 and 3 to make six print No. 1 hexagon pieces total.

[5] Repeat steps 2 and 3 to make one print No. 2 hexagon piece.

[6] Aligning edges to be joined, place two print No. 1 hexagon pieces right sides together. Pin pieces together at center (**Photo 4**).

[7] With a single strand of quilting thread, begin stitching about ⅛" from one corner using tiny whipstitches and catching a thread of both fabric folds (**Photo 5**). You'll feel the paper templates with your needle, but do not stitch through them.

[8] Backstitch to nearest corner (**Photo 6**).

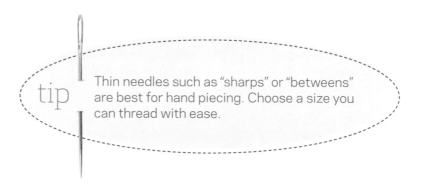

tip    Thin needles such as "sharps" or "betweens" are best for hand piecing. Choose a size you can thread with ease.

PHOTO 8

PHOTO 9

PHOTO 10

PHOTO 11

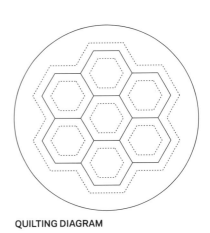

QUILTING DIAGRAM

[9] Once you reach the corner, reverse direction of stitching and sew across edges to opposite corner (**Photo 7**). Take a backstitch, and knot thread.

[10] Lightly press open joined pieces and check seam from right side (**Photo 8**). Stitches should not show. If they do, take smaller whipstitches through less of the fabric folds as you sew.

[11] To set in print No. 2 hexagon piece, pin and sew seam on one side. Reposition stitched pieces so next seam is aligned and continue sewing, bending hexagon piece as needed (**Photo 9**).

[12] When all pieces have been joined, press to set edges. Pull basting threads and remove templates from the back to make hexagon appliqué (**photos 10** and **11**).

## appliqué coaster

[1] Center wrong side of hexagon appliqué on right side of one print No. 2—9" square. Secure with small safety pins.

[2] Use matching thread to hand-appliqué outer edge of hexagon appliqué in place.

## finish coaster

[1] Layer appliquéd square, batting, and backing. (For details, see Quilt It, *page 197*)

[2] Quilt as desired. The coasters shown are echo-quilted by hand a scant ¼" from inside and outside edges of each hexagon (**Quilting Diagram**).

[3] Center Pattern B over quilted square; cut out circle.

[4] Fold print No. 2 bias binding strip in half lengthwise, wrong sides together.

[5] Aligning edges of binding strip with coaster's curved raw edge, sew binding to coaster using ¼" seam, easing in extra fabric around curve. Join ends to fit, then trim excess binding. Turn binding to wrong side of coaster. Hand-stitch binding in place to complete one coaster.

3

DESIGNER **CINDY TAYLOR OATES**
PHOTOGRAPHS **CAMERON SADEGHPOUR**

# apron
## strings

Whip up an easy retro cover-up with sweet girly ruffles and bows to make a fashion statement in the kitchen or out on the town.

*Aprons are back, and fun to wear both in and out of kitchen. The large panel is the perfect place to show-off your style with a colorful, large-scale print.*

## materials

**Apron - View 1**

▸ ¾ yard pink-and-green floral (apron, waistband, pocket)
▸ ⅜ yard pink print (ties, piping)
▸ ¾ yard multicolor stripe (ruffle, pocket ruffle)
▸ Lightweight, non-fusible interfacing

**Apron - View 2**

▸ ¾ yard blue large print (apron, ties)
▸ ½ yard multicolor large dot (waistband, ruffle)
▸ 5 yards medium-wide blue rickrack
▸ Lightweight, non-fusible interfacing

**Apron - View 3**

▸ 1½ yards aqua print (apron body, waistband, ruffle, pocket, ties)
▸ ⅝ yard brown print (bias trim)
▸ Lightweight, non-fusible interfacing

Finished aprons:
Apron - View 1
Width at waistband: 25" Length: 21"
Apron - View 2
Width at waistband: 25" Length: 23"
Apron - View 3
Width at waistband: 24" Length: 22"

**Quantities** are for 44/45"-wide, 100% cotton fabrics.
**Measurements** include a ¼" seam allowance. Sew with right sides together unless otherwise stated.

## cut fabrics for apron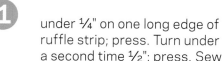

To make the best use of your fabrics, cut pieces in the following order. Patterns can be found on *Pattern Sheet 2.*

**From pink-and-green floral, cut:**

▸ 1 of Apron Pattern (View 1)
▸ 1—7" square (lower pocket)
▸ 1—3½×26" strip (waistband)
▸ 1—3½×7" rectangle (upper pocket)

**From pink print, cut:**

▸ 2—3½×30" strips (ties)
▸ 1—2×37" strip (piping)
▸ 1—2×6½" strip (pocket piping)

**From multicolor stripe, cut:**

▸ 1—4¾×42" strip (ruffle)
▸ 1—4¾×10" strip (ruffle)
▸ 1—2¾×10" strip (pocket ruffle)

**From interfacing, cut:**

▸ 1—1½×7" rectangle

## assemble apron body

[1] To sew darts in apron piece, match up dashed lines, then stitch. Press darts toward center front (**Diagram 1**).

[2] With wrong sides together, fold pink print 2×37" piping strip in half lengthwise; press. Matching raw edges, sew folded strip to lower edge of apron.

[3] Join multicolor stripe 4¾×42" and 4¾×10" ruffle strips together along one short edge to make one long ruffle strip. Turn

under ¼" on one long edge of ruffle strip; press. Turn under a second time ½"; press. Sew through all layers close to the first folded edge.

[4] With a long machine stitch, sew ½" from long raw edge of ruffle strip. Pull up threads to gather the edge.

[5] With raw edges aligned, match center of gathered strip with bottom center of apron. Pin and stitch with ½" seam allowance (**Diagram 2**). Finish raw edges of seam with a machine zigzag stitch. Press seam toward apron.

[6] Turn under ¼" on each side edge of apron and ruffle; press. Turn under a second time ½" and press. Sew through all layers close to first folded edge.

## make ties

[1] Turn under ¼" twice on each long edge of pink print 3½×30" strip; press. Sew through all layers close to first folded edge.

[2] Fold hemmed strip in half lengthwise and sew across one end. Clip point. Press seam to one side. Turn right side out and press seam in center of hemmed strip. Sew across resulting triangle (**Diagram 3**).

[3] In the center of each raw end of the strip, make a fold so the strip end is 1¼" wide. Pin in place, then sew across fold to complete an apron tie (**Diagram 4**).

[4] Repeat steps 1 through 3 with remaining pink print 3½×30" strip to make a second apron tie.

## make waistband

[1] With wrong sides together, press pink-and-green floral 3½×26" strip in half lengthwise. Open up strip and press under ¼" along one long edge.

[2] Sew unpressed edge of waistband strip to upper edge of apron. (Waistband should extend ½" beyond each apron edge.) Press seam toward waistband.

[3] Position raw ends of apron ties on waistband just below fold. Then fold waistband on previous fold with right sides together and long edges matching. Sew ties to

ends of waistband with ½" seam allowance (even with finished side edges of apron). Turn waistband and ties right side out; press.

[4] Pin pressed edge of waistband to wrong side of apron; slip-stitch in place. Topstitch waistband close to bottom edge.

## make and add pocket

[1] Fold pink print 2×6½" pocket piping strip in half lengthwise. Sew across ends. Clip corners, turn right side out, and press.

[2] Fold under ¼" twice on lower edge and ends of multicolor stripe 2¾×10" pocket ruffle strip. Press. Sew close to first folded edge.

[3] With a long machine stitch, sew ¼" from unhemmed edge of pocket ruffle strip. Pull up threads to gather the edge.

[4] With wrong side of ruffle on right side of pocket, center piping and ruffle on one edge of pink-and-green floral lower pocket; stitch in place (**Diagram 5**).

[5] Aligning long edges, place interfacing on wrong side of pink-and-green floral upper pocket. Turn under ½" along opposite pocket edge and press. Sew upper pocket to lower pocket; press seam toward upper pocket (**Diagram 6**).

[6] Fold upper pocket in half with right sides together, matching pressed edge with seam. Sew side edges with ½" seam allowance (**Diagram 7**). Clip corners, turn right side out, and press. Press under ½" on edges of lower pocket.

[7] Referring to pattern for placement, pin pocket to apron. Edgestitch pocket to apron, keeping ruffle and piping free from stitching.

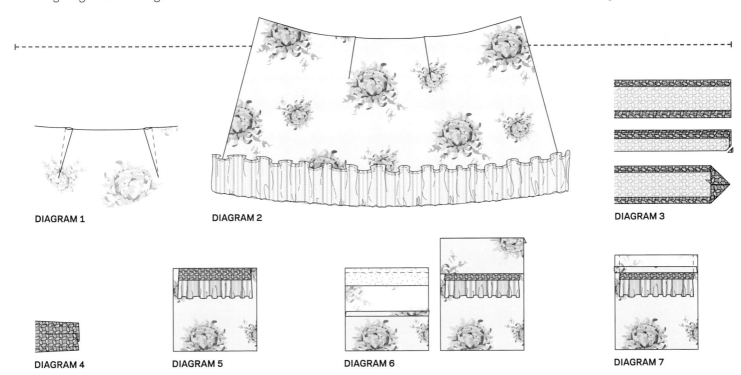

DIAGRAM 1

DIAGRAM 2

DIAGRAM 3

DIAGRAM 4

DIAGRAM 5

DIAGRAM 6

DIAGRAM 7

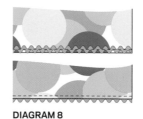

**DIAGRAM 8**

## cut fabrics for apron ②

**From blue large print, cut:**
▸ 1 of Apron Pattern (View 2)
▸ 2—3½×30" strips (ties)

**From multicolor large dot, cut:**
▸ 2 of Waistband Pattern
▸ 1—6½×42" strip (ruffle)
▸ 1—6½×10" strip (ruffle)

**From interfacing, cut:**
▸ 1 of Waistband Pattern

## assemble apron body

[1] Referring to Assemble Apron Body on *page 76*, Step 1, sew darts in apron piece.

[2] Using ½" seam allowance, join large dot 6½×42" and 6½×10" ruffle strips along one short edge to make one long ruffle strip.

[3] Machine-zigzag-stitch one long edge of ruffle strip. Place rickrack on right side of fabric along stitched edge. Sew through center of rickrack. Fold edge of fabric and rickrack to wrong side; press. Topstitch 3/16" from folded edge through all layers (**Diagram 8**).

[4] Referring to Assemble Apron Body on *page 76*, steps 4 and 5, gather one long edge of ruffle strip and sew to bottom of apron.

[5] Center rickrack over seam between ruffle and apron body. Sew through center of rickrack using matching thread.

[6] Turn under ¼" twice on each side edge of apron and ruffle; press. Sew through all layers close to first folded edge.

**DIAGRAM 9**

**DIAGRAM 10**

## make ties

Referring to Make Ties on *page 76*, steps 1 through 4, use blue large print 3½×30" strips, to make apron ties.

## make waistband

[1] Place interfacing on wrong side of a large dot waistband piece; stitch in place close to raw edges.

[2] Aligning edge of rickrack with raw edges of interfaced waistband piece, join rickrack to upper and lower edges of right side (**Diagram 9**).

[3] Turn under ¼" on bottom edge of remaining waistband piece; press.

[4] Sew waistband pieces together along upper curved edge; clip curves.

[5] Join the waistband edge with rickrack to apron (**Diagram 10**). (Waistband should extend ½" beyond each apron edge.) Press seam toward waistband.

[6] Position raw ends of apron ties on waistband just below seam. Fold waistband on seam with right sides together. Sew through all layers with ½" seam allowance (even with finished side edges of apron). Turn waistband and ties right side out; press.

[7] Topstitch waistband ¼" from edges.

## cut fabrics for apron ③

**From aqua print, cut:**
- 1—20×24" rectangle, cutting it into enough 4¼"-wide bias strips to total 90" for ruffle (For details, see Cutting on the Bias, *page 203*.)
- 1 of Apron Pattern (View 3)
- 2—3½×30" strips (ties)
- 2 of Waistband Pattern
- 1 of Upper Pocket Pattern
- 1 of Lower Pocket Pattern

**From brown print, cut:**
- 1¼×19" bias strip for bow
- 1—12" square, cutting it into enough 1⅛"-wide bias strips to total 90" for trim

**From lightweight interfacing, cut:**
- 1 of Waistband Pattern
- 1—1¾×6½" strip

## assemble apron body

[1] Referring to Assemble Apron Body on *page 76*, Step 1, sew darts in apron piece.

[2] Cut and piece aqua print 4¼"-wide bias strips to make one 90"-long ruffle strip. Turn under a scant ¼" twice on one long edge of ruffle strip; press. Sew through all layers close to first folded edge.

[3] With a long machine stitch, sew ¼" from long raw edge of ruffle strip. Pull up threads to gather the edge.

[4] With wrong sides together, match center of gathered ruffle strip and bottom center of apron; pin strip along bottom and side edges, evenly distributing gathers. Stitch in place; do not press ruffle strip open.

[5] Cut and piece brown print 1⅛"-wide bias strips to make:
- 1—55"-long bias strip
- 1—26"-long bias strip
- 1—7"-long bias strip

## modern twist

If ruffles aren't your thing, try pairing turquoise paisley prints and a contrasting polka-dot bound edge for a more contemporary flair. A simple U-shape pocket featuring the same binding as the apron edge finishes off the apron.

[6] With the bias strip right side down, pin and stitch brown print 55"-long bias strip to apron edge over the ruffle (**Diagram 11**). Press ruffle and bias strip away from apron, then press bias strip away from ruffle.

[7] Tuck raw edge of bias behind the seam allowance and pin in place. Sew close to folded edge of bias through all layers.

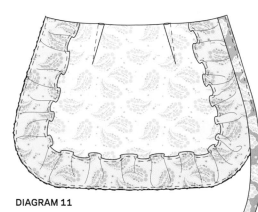

**DIAGRAM 11**

## make ties

Referring to Make Ties on *page 76*, steps 1 through 4, use aqua print 3½×30" strips to make apron ties.

## make waistband

[1] Baste waistband interfacing to wrong side of an aqua print waistband piece. Join waistband pieces along upper curved edge. Clip curves, turn right side out, and press.

[2] Position raw ends of apron ties on waistband just below seam. Fold waistband along seam with right sides together (**Diagram 12**). Sew through all layers with ½" seam allowance. Turn waistband and ties right side out; press. Topstitch waistband ¼" from finished edges.

[3] With wrong sides together, sew waistband to apron.

[4] With right sides together, sew brown print 26"-long bias strip to upper edge of apron, extending bias strip ½" beyond finished edges of waistband (**Diagram 13**). Press waistband and bias strip away from apron.

[5] Fold and stitch bias around seam allowance as in Assemble Apron Body, Step 7.

## make and add pocket

[1] Baste 1¾×6½" interfacing strip on wrong side of aqua print upper pocket's straight edge. With wrong sides together, join straight edges of upper and lower pocket pieces. With the bias strip right side down, pin and stitch brown print 7"-long bias strip to joined pocket edges (**Diagram 14**). Press upper pocket and bias strip away from lower pocket.

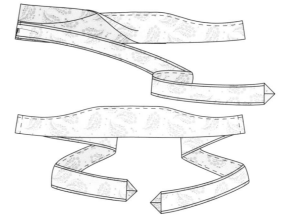

**DIAGRAM 12**

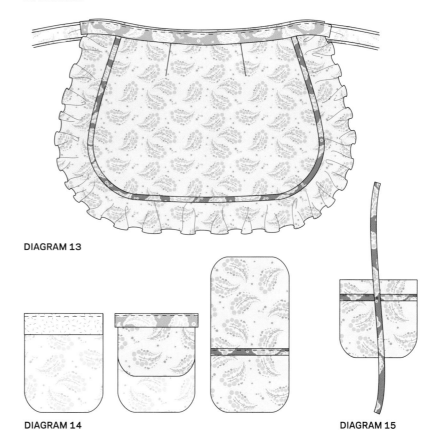

**DIAGRAM 13**

**DIAGRAM 14**

**DIAGRAM 15**

[2] Fold and stitch bias around seam allowance as in Assemble Apron Body, Step 7.

[3] Fold pieced pocket in half with right sides together. Sew together, leaving an opening along one side. Clip corners and curves, turn right side out, and press. Slipstitch opening closed.

[4] Fold 1¼×19" bias strip in half lengthwise. Sew together along long edges to make a tube, then turn right side out and press. Join center of tube to center of apron pocket (**Diagram 15**). Tie tube into bow.

[5] Referring to pattern for placement, pin pocket to apron. Edgestitch pocket to apron.

# all about stripes

DESIGNER **PAT SLOAN**
PHOTOGRAPHS **GREG SCHEIDEMANN**

Hesitant to work with stripes? Try this simple
trick and every stripe will fall right in line.

Here's a sure-fire way to get all the stripes of this yummy table runner going in the same direction. It's a simple technique, but oh, so dramatic when all the blocks are sewn together. Just draw a diagonal pencil line, carefully layer the squares, check, sew, press, and repeat. You'll master the method in no time.

## materials

- ⅜ yard pink stripe (triangle-squares)
- ⅝ yard pink print (triangle-squares, inner border, binding)
- ½ yard brown print (setting and corner triangles, outer border)
- ¾ yard backing fabric
- 26×47" thin quilt batting

Finished table runner: 19¼×40½"
Finished triangle-square: 3" square

Quantities are for 44/45"-wide, 100% cotton fabrics. Measurements include ¼" seam allowances. Sew with right sides together unless otherwise stated.

## cut fabrics

Cut pieces in the following order.

**From pink stripe, cut:**
- 19—3⅞" squares

**From pink print, cut:**
- 3—2½×42" binding strips
- 2—1×34½" inner border strips
- 2—1×14¼" inner border strips
- 19—3⅞" squares

**From brown print, cut:**
- 2—3×35½" outer border strips
- 2—3×19¼" outer border strips
- 2—5⅛" squares, cutting each in half diagonally for 4 corner triangles total
- 4—5½" squares, cutting each diagonally twice in an X for 16 setting triangles total (you will use 14)

## assemble triangle-squares

[1] Use a pencil to mark a diagonal line on wrong side of each pink stripe 3⅞" square (**Diagram 1**); see Stripe Trick. (To prevent fabric from stretching, place 220-grit sandpaper under squares.)

[2] Layer each marked pink stripe square atop a pink print 3⅞" square. Sew each pair together with two seams, stitching ¼" on each side of drawn line (**Diagram 2**).

[3] Cut a pair apart on drawn line to make two triangle units (**Diagram 3**). Press each triangle unit open, pressing seam toward pink print, to make two triangle-squares. Each triangle-square should be 3½" square including seam allowances. Repeat to make 38 triangle-squares total (you will use 37).

**DIAGRAM 1**     **DIAGRAM 2**

**DIAGRAM 3**

## assemble table runner center

[1] Referring to **Table Runner Assembly Diagram**, lay out triangle-squares and 14 setting triangles in diagonal rows.

[2] Sew together pieces in each row. Press seams in one direction,

**TABLE RUNNER ASSEMBLY DIAGRAM**

alternating direction with each row. Join rows; press seams in one direction. Add brown print corner triangles to make table runner center; press seams toward corner triangles. The table runner center should be 13¼×34½" including seam allowances.

## add borders

[1] Sew long inner border strips to long edges of table runner center. Add short inner border strips to remaining edges. Press all seams toward inner border.

[2] Sew long outer border strips to long edges of table runner center. Add short outer border strips to remaining edges to complete table runner top. Press all seams toward outer border.

## finish table runner

[1] Layer table runner top, batting, and backing; baste. (For details, see Quilt It, page 197.)

[2] Quilt as desired. Pat machine-quilted a curvy line through the triangle-squares and a leaf design in the outer border.

[3] Bind with pink print binding strips. (For details, see Better Binding, *page 206*.) Pat used a narrow machine blanket stitch to attach the binding on her table runner.

tip Punch up a plain-Jane block with a stripe fabric. Stripes can add directional movement (like the diagonal slant on this table runner) or an off-beat twist when cut on the bias for a border or binding.

## stripe trick

Puzzled by how to get stripes to run in the same direction in blocks time after time? Designer Pat Sloan shares her trick for marking and sewing stripe fabrics and guarantees success with her easy approach.

As you mark stripe fabric, make certain stripes of each square are running in the same direction and that the line you draw always runs the same way on the fabric. This ensures that all stripes are going in the same direction after sewing (**Photo 1**).

PHOTO 1

Layer a marked pink stripe square atop a pink print square. Sew the pair together with two seams, stitching ¼" on each side of drawn line. Cut the pair apart on drawn line to make two triangle units (**Photo 2**).

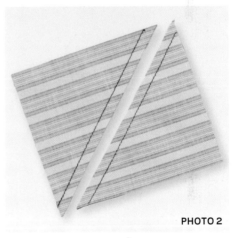
PHOTO 2

Press each triangle unit open, pressing seam toward pink print, to make two triangle-squares (**Photo 3**).

PHOTO 3

# topthis

QUILTMAKER **KATE HARDY**
PHOTOGRAPHS **GREG SCHEIDEMANN**

Frame a lively fabric with Four-Patch units and add a border print in a different colorway for a can't-miss table mat.

*Satisfy your chocolate craving with a no-calorie table topper made from trendy prints. It's sure to liven up coffee time, and your friends will never suspect how easy it is to construct.*

## materials

- ▸ 9×22" piece (fat eighth) blue swirl print (Four-Patch units)
- ▸ 9×22" piece (fat eighth) brown dot (Four-Patch units)
- ▸ ⅜ yard brown leaf print (Four-Patch units, binding)
- ▸ 9×22" piece (fat eighth) blue diamond print (Four-Patch units)
- ▸ 18×22" piece (fat quarter) lime green floral (center rectangle)
- ▸ ⅞ yard brown floral (outer border)
- ▸ ⅞ yard backing fabric
- ▸ 28×34" batting

Finished table mat: 21½×27½"

Quantities are for 44/45"-wide, 100% cotton fabrics. Measurements include ¼" seam allowances. Sew with right sides together unless otherwise stated.

## cut fabrics

Cut pieces in the following order.

**From blue swirl print, cut:**
- ▸ 2—2×21" strips

**From brown dot, cut:**
- ▸ 2—2×21" strips

**From brown leaf print, cut:**
- ▸ 3—2½×42" binding strips
- ▸ 2—2×21" strips

**From blue diamond print, cut:**
- ▸ 2—2×21" strips

**From lime green floral, cut:**
- ▸ 1—9½×15½" rectangle

**From brown floral, cut:**
- ▸ 2—3½×32½" outer border strips
- ▸ 2—3½×27½" outer border strips

**tip**

If you want to expand your skill set before quilting the inner and outer borders of this table topper, practice free-motion quilting in the center panel. The small area is ideal for experimenting with curved lines and designs.

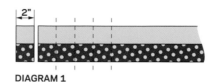

**DIAGRAM 1**                    **DIAGRAM 2**

## assemble four-patch units

[1] Sew together a blue swirl print 2×21" strip and a brown dot 2×21" strip to make a strip set (**Diagram 1**). Press seam toward brown dot strip. Repeat to make a second strip set. Cut strip sets into twenty 2"-wide A segments total.

[2] Repeat Step 1 using brown leaf print 2×21" strips and blue diamond print 2×21" strips to make twenty 2"-wide B segments.

[3] Sew together an A segment and a B segment to make a Four-Patch unit (**Diagram 2**). Press seam in one direction. The Four-Patch unit should be 3½" square including seam allowances. Repeat to make 20 Four-Patch units total.

## assemble quilt top

[1] Referring to **Quilt Assembly Diagram**, sew together five Four-Patch units in a row to make an inner border strip. Press seams in one direction. Repeat to make four inner border strips total.

[2] Sew two inner border strips to long edges of lime green floral 9½×15½" rectangle. Sew remaining inner border strips to remaining edges of rectangle to make quilt center. Press all seams toward rectangle. The quilt center should be 15½×21½" including seam allowances.

**QUILT ASSEMBLY DIAGRAM**

[3] Aligning midpoints, sew short brown floral outer border strips to short edges of quilt center, beginning and ending seams ¼" from corners. Add long brown floral outer border strips to remaining edges, mitering corners, to complete quilt top. (For details, see Mitering Borders, *page 208*.) Press all seams toward outer border.

## finish quilt

[1] Layer quilt top, batting, and backing; baste. (For details, see Quilt It, *page 197*.)

[2] Quilt as desired. This quilt is stitched in the ditch of the center rectangle and the inner and outer borders.

[3] Bind with brown leaf print binding strips. (For details, see Better Binding, *page 206*.)

# everyday
# elegance

The secret to this striking place mat set is the fabric choice—
myriad neutrals in a variety of shades.  PHOTOGRAPHS **GREG SCHEIDEMANN**

*Just eight Flying Geese blocks make up the center of these simple-to-sew place mats.*

*Make a flock of blocks, then stitch them together, assembly-line fashion. Before you know it, you'll have a set made for yourself or to give as a gift. Choose a favorite color, then select assorted medium and light prints of the same hue to achieve this understated look.*

## materials
## for four place mats

- ⅜ yard total assorted cream prints (blocks)
- 1⅓ yards total assorted tan prints (blocks, border)
- ⅝ yard light cream print (binding)
- 1 yard backing fabric
- 4—17×21" rectangles batting

Finished place mat: 12½×16½"
Finished block: 3½×6½"

Quantities are for 44/45"-wide, 100% cotton fabrics. Measurements include ¼" seam allowances. Sew with right sides together unless otherwise stated.

## cut fabrics

Cut pieces in the following order.

**From assorted cream prints, cut:**
- 8—3½×6½" rectangles
- 20—3½" squares

**From assorted tan prints, cut:**
- 8—2½×12½" border strips
- 24—3½×6½" rectangles
- 44—3½" squares

**From light cream print, cut:**
- 7—2½×42" binding strips

From backing fabric, cut:
- 4—17×21" rectangles

tip  Experiment with place mat design by rearranging the Flying Geese units. Try turning them in different directions for a completely new look.

## assemble
## flying geese blocks

[1] Use a pencil to mark a diagonal line on wrong side of each assorted cream and tan print 3½" square. (To prevent fabric from stretching as you draw lines, place 220-grit sandpaper under each square.)

[2] Referring to **Diagram 1**, align a marked cream or tan print square with one end of an assorted cream or tan print 3½×6½" rectangle; note placement of marked line. Sew on marked line. Trim excess fabric, leaving a ¼" seam allowance. Press open attached triangle.

[3] Repeat Step 2, sewing a marked cream or tan print square to opposite end of cream or tan print rectangle, to make a Flying Geese block (**Diagram 2**). The block should be 3½×6½" including seam allowances.

[4] Repeat steps 2 and 3 to make 32 Flying Geese blocks total.

**DIAGRAM 1**

**DIAGRAM 2**

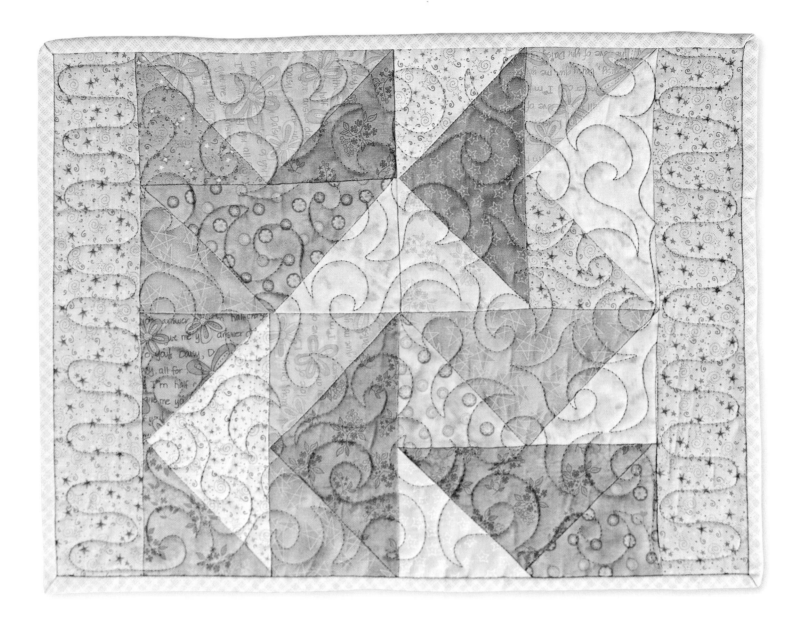

## assemble and finish place mats

[1] Referring to photo above, lay out eight Flying Geese blocks in four pairs. Join blocks in each pair; press seams in one direction. Sew together pairs in each row; press seams in opposite directions. Join rows to make a place mat center. Press seam in one direction.

[2] Join assorted tan print 2½×12½" border strips to opposite edges of place mat center to make a place mat top. Press seams toward border.

[3] Layer place mat top with 17×21" rectangles of batting and backing; baste. (For details, see Quilt It, *page 197.*)

[4] Quilt as desired. The place mats are machine-quilted with an allover flame design in each place mat center and a wave pattern in the border.

[5] Bind with light cream print binding strips. (For details, see Better Binding, *page 206.*)

[6] Repeat steps 1 through 5 to make four place mats total.

99

102

95

110

(92)

(115)

# carry on

There's something about a great bag that's hard to resist. Whether it's a place for everyday necessities, a music player, books, or an assortment of loose papers, you'll find just the bag you need in this collection to corral it all.

**Pick a Pocket** ...................................92
**Over the Top** ....................................95
**Mod Music** .......................................99
**Messenger Bag** .............................. 102
**Holds It All** ..................................... 106
**Check It Out** ................................... 110
**Style File** ........................................ 115

# pick a pocket

DESIGNER **MONICA SOLORIO-SNOW**
PHOTOGRAPHS **ADAM ALBRIGHT**

A simple bag cleverly incorporates six outer pockets for everyday necessities.

*This simple-to-sew bag offers six slender exterior pockets— handy places to keep hard-to-find items—and a roomy interior. The sew-simple trick is that the pockets are formed when the straps are sewn on the bag pieces.*

## materials

- ¼ yard blue print (straps)
- ⅔ yard blue-and-green print (pockets)
- ⅔ yard green print (bag/lining)
- 2—10¼×14½" rectangles thin, firm batting

Finished bag: 8×10×4"

Quantities are for 44/45"-wide, 100% cotton fabrics. Measurements include ¼" seam allowances. Sew with right sides together unless otherwise stated.

## cut fabrics

Cut pieces in the following order.

**From blue print, cut:**
- 2—4×34½" strips

**From blue-and-green print, cut:**
- 2—14½×16½" rectangles

**From green print, cut:**
- 2—14½×20½" rectangles

## assemble straps

[1] Fold and press a blue print 4×34½" strip in half lengthwise with wrong side inside (Diagram 1).

[2] Open and press long edges to center. Refold in half and press. Topstitch ⅛" from outer edges to make a strap (Diagram 1).

[3] Repeat steps 1 and 2 to make a second strap.

## assemble bag

[1] Fold and press one blue-and-green print 14½×16½" rectangle in half lengthwise with wrong side inside to make an 8¼×14½" pocket rectangle. Repeat with remaining blue-and-green print rectangle to make a second pocket rectangle.

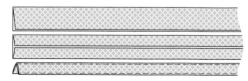

**DIAGRAM 1**

[2] Referring to **Diagram 2**, layer a green print 14½×20½" lining rectangle and a pocket rectangle, right sides together. Place a 10¼×14½" batting rectangle under the layered pieces; pin all layers together.

[3] Referring to **Diagram 2**, pin a strap to the bottom edge of layered pieces, leaving 4" between strap sides.

[4] Place a pin on each side of strap 10¼" from bottom edge. Beginning at bottom edge of layered pieces, topstitch one side of strap up to the pin marking 10¼"; remove pin, sew across strap, and topstitch back down to bottom edge. Repeat with remaining side of strap to complete one bag unit.

[5] Repeat steps 2 through 4 to make a second bag unit.

[6] Layer bag units right sides together; pin. Pin loose portion of straps in place to prevent catching them in stitching. Join units around all edges,

## color option

All it takes are three favorite prints to make this easy-to-sew bag. If you're feeling daring, create a black-and-white version with a pop of red for the upper band.

leaving a 5" opening at top center for turning (**Diagram 3**). Press seams open.

[7] To shape flat bottom for bag, at one corner match bottom seam line to side seam line, creating a flattened triangle (**Diagram 4**). Measuring 2" from point of triangle, draw a 4"-long line

across triangle. Sew on drawn line. Trim excess fabric. Repeat with remaining bottom corner of bag, and both corners of green print lining.

[8] Turn bag to right side and finger-press seams. Slip-stitch lining opening closed. Insert lining into bag.

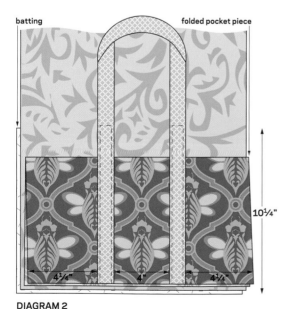

batting     folded pocket piece

10¼"

4¼"    4"    4¼"

**DIAGRAM 2**

**DIAGRAM 3**

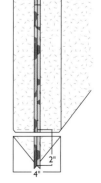

2"

4"

**DIAGRAM 4**

# over
## the top

DESIGNER **ELIZABETH STUMBO**
PHOTOGRAPHS **ADAM ALBRIGHT**

Your purse should reflect your style.
Stitch and finish this one in the morning;
grab it and go in the afternoon.

*Keep it simple or fancy it up. This one-handle tote is so simple, you can create one to match every outfit. All you need are three coordinating fabrics and some fusible interfacing to stiffen the sides and bottom of the bag.*

## materials

- ⅓ yard green print (lining)
- ⅓ yard green-and-aqua-floral (bag)
- ¼ yard brown-and-green print (handle)
- ¾ yard stiff, fusible interfacing
- Magnetic snap closure

Finished bag: 12½×5½×3"

Quantities are for 44/45"-wide, 100% cotton fabrics. Measurements include ¼" seam allowances. Sew with right sides together unless otherwise stated.

## cut fabrics

Cut pieces in the following order. Pattern can be found on *Pattern Sheet 1*.

**From green print, cut:**
- 2 of Bag Pattern for lining
- 1—3½×13" rectangle
- 2—3½×6¼" rectangles

**From green-and-aqua floral, cut:**
- 2 of Bag Pattern
- 1—3½×13" rectangle
- 2—3½×6¼" rectangles

**From brown-and-green print, cut:**
- 1—4×23" strip

**From stiff, fusible interfacing, cut:**
- 2 of Bag Pattern
- 2—1×23" strips
- 1—3½×13" rectangle
- 2—3½×6¼" rectangles
- 2—2" squares

## assemble bag lining

[1] Place each green print lining piece wrong side up. Center interfacing 2" square ¼" below top edge on each lining piece. Following manufacturer's instructions, press in place to reinforce fabric where closure will be placed.

[2] Following manufacturer's instructions, attach one half of magnetic closure to each lining piece, centering closure ⅞" from top edge.

[3] Sew green print 3½×6¼" rectangles to edges of green print lining piece, ending stitches ¼" from bottom edge (**Diagram 1**). In same manner, join remaining green print lining piece to remaining long edges of green print rectangles (**Diagram 2**). Press all seams open.

[4] Join green print 3½×13" rectangle to bottom edge of Step 3 unit, leaving an 8" opening along one edge, to make bag lining (**Diagram 3**). Press seams open.

**DIAGRAM 1**

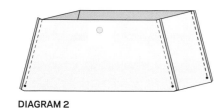

**DIAGRAM 2**

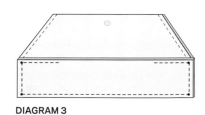

**DIAGRAM 3**

## assemble bag body

[1] Press a fusible interfacing bag piece onto wrong side of each green-and-aqua floral bag piece. Fuse interfacing 3½×13" rectangle to wrong side of corresponding green-and-aqua floral rectangle; and an interfacing 3½×6¼" rectangle to wrong side of each corresponding green-and-aqua floral rectangle.

[2] Fold and press green-and-aqua floral 3½×6¼" rectangle in half lengthwise with right side inside. Unfold, and using crease as a guide, topstitch 5" from top edge, then continue stitching from center of rectangle to both bottom corners (**Diagram 4**).

[3] Referring to Assemble Bag Lining, Step 3, sew together green-and-aqua floral bag pieces and 3½×6¼" rectangles. Press seams open and topstitch on both sides of seam.

[4] Join green-and-aqua floral 3½×13" rectangle to bottom edge of Step 3 unit, leaving a 1" opening along each long edge for handle insertion to make bag body; see Bag Pattern for placement of opening. Press seams open. Turn bag right side out.

## assemble handle

[1] Fold and press brown-and-green print 4×23" strip in half lengthwise with wrong side inside (**Diagram 5**).

[2] Open and press long edges to center. Refold in half and press. Unfold and insert an interfacing 1×23" strip into each fold. Fuse in place. Refold strip in half again to make a 1×23" strip. Topstitch ⅛" from outer edges to make handle (**Diagram 5**).

## finish bag

[1] Insert bag body into bag lining right sides together, matching seams; pin. Sew together bag body and bag lining (**Diagram 6**).

**DIAGRAM 4**

**DIAGRAM 5**

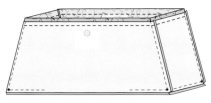

**DIAGRAM 6**

tip

Follow the instructions that come with your fusible interfacing to ensure you are using the correct iron temperature setting and know whether to use a dry or steam iron. Following the recommended time for pressing is critical to obtain a secure, bubble-free bond between fusible interfacing and fabric.

[2] Turn bag to right side through opening in lining and finger-press seams. Slip-stitch opening closed. Insert lining into bag; press. Topstitch ⅛" from upper edge.

[3] Referring to **Diagram 7**, insert ½" of handle ends into front and back openings at bag bottom; pin. Beginning at bottom edge of bag and handle, topstitch ¼" from one side of handle to secure to bag, sew length of handle, and topstitch back down to opposite bottom edge through bag and handle. Repeat with remaining side of handle.

[4] Slip-stitch handle openings closed.

[5] Turn the bag lining side out. Fold bag side in half along topstitching line. Stitch a ¼"-wide dart in fold, tapering to side edge 1" below top edge (**Diagram 8**). Turn bag right side out.

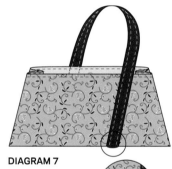

**DIAGRAM 7**

**DIAGRAM 8**

1"

DESIGNER **DEB JENSEN**
PHOTOGRAPHS **GREG SCHEIDEMANN**

# mod music

Tuckaway pockets protect tune players and ear buds in a simple clip-on carrier.

*With a swivel hook that snaps onto jeans or totes, this MP3 player holder will let you take your music with you—in a fashionable way. You'll want to make oodles for gifts or fashion accessories in today's bright paisleys, polka dots, or florals.*

## materials

▸ ¼ yard green print (bag fabric, lining)
▸ ¼ yard fusible interfacing
▸ 4×6" rectangle batting
▸ ¾"-long swivel hook
▸ ¾"-diameter button

**Finished project:** 3×5×½"

**Quantities** are for 44/45"-wide, 100% cotton fabrics.
**Measurements** include ⅜" seam allowances unless otherwise stated. Sew with right sides together unless otherwise stated.

## cut fabrics

To make the best use of your fabrics, cut pieces in the following order. Pattern can be found on *Pattern Sheet 2*. To make a template of the pattern, see "What Are Templates?" on *page 201*.

**From green print, cut:**
- 4—4×6" rectangles
- 1—4×4¼" rectangle
- 2 of Flap Pattern
- 1—2¼" square
- 1—2×3" rectangle

**From fusible interfacing, cut:**
- 2—4×6" rectangles

**From batting, cut:**
- 1 of Flap Pattern

## assemble bag body

[1] Turn under ¼" on one short edge of green print 4×4¼" rectangle; press. Turn under again ½"; press. Sew through all layers ⅜" from second folded edge to make outer pocket (**Diagram 1**).

[2] Place outer pocket atop one green print 4×6" rectangle, right sides up; baste (**Diagram 2**).

[3] Fuse a 4×6" rectangle of interfacing to wrong side of one green print 4×6" rectangle to make an interfaced rectangle. Repeat to make a second interfaced rectangle. (Using interfacing will help the bag retain its shape.)

[4] Referring to **Diagram 3**, join outer pocket piece to one interfaced rectangle along side and bottom edges to make bag body.

[5] To shape flat bottom for bag, at one corner, match bottom seam line to side seam line, creating a flattened triangle (**Diagram 4**). Measuring ⅜" from point of triangle, draw a line across triangle. Sew on drawn line. Trim excess fabric. Repeat with remaining bottom corner

to make bag body. Turn bag body right side out.

## assemble lining

Referring to Assemble Bag Body steps 4 and 5, sew together remaining green print 4×6" rectangle and interfaced rectangle, leaving a 2¾"-wide opening at bottom, to make lining. Do not turn right side out.

## assemble bag flap

[1] Fold green print 2×3" rectangle in half lengthwise; sew together long edges with ¼" seam. Turn right side out and press to make button strip. Aligning raw edges, place ends of button strip side by side at bottom center of a green print flap piece (**Diagram 5**); baste.

[2] Place batting on wrong side of remaining green print flap piece; baste. Join two bag flaps together

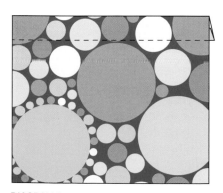

**DIAGRAM 1**

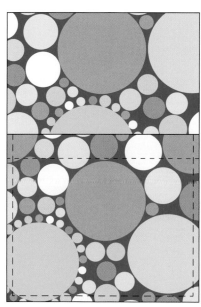

**DIAGRAM 2**

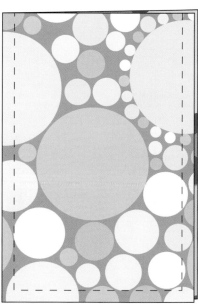

**DIAGRAM 3**

## color option

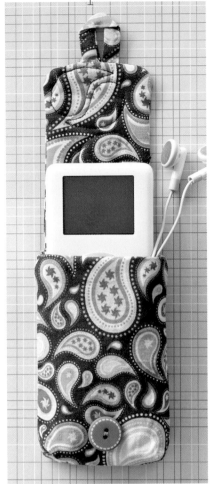

**tip** A mechanical pencil always keeps a sharp point, so it's a good choice for marking placement lines on an appliqué foundation or tracing around templates on fabric.

Requiring just a ¼" yard of fabric, this project is ideal for using up fabric scraps or indulging in a favorite designer fabric. With so many wonderful fabric options available, it's a snap to match this music holder to any bag or outfit. And embellishing it is fun, too. Whether you find a single button you can't resist buying or use an orphaned one you've saved, it's a great way to showcase a snazzy button.

along sides and curved end to make bag flap. Turn right side out.

[3] Quilt as desired. Deb machine-quilted the flap of this portable media player bag with diagonal lines spaced 1" apart.

## assemble swivel hook strap

[1] Fold green print 2¼" square in half; join long edges with ¼" seam. Turn strap right side out to make swivel hook strap.

[2] Thread strap through swivel hook ring; fold strap in half. Baste ends together.

[3] Align raw edges of strap ends along upper edge of bag back (**Diagram 6**); baste.

## finish bag

[1] Center straight edge of bag flap along upper edge of bag back atop swivel hook strap; baste.

[2] Slip bag inside lining, matching side seams; pin. (The flap, swivel hook, and strap are sandwiched between bag and lining.) Sew upper edges together.

[3] Turn bag right side out through opening in lining bottom. Slip-stitch opening closed. Insert lining into bag. Press upper edges of bag.

[4] Sew button on bag front.

**³⁄₈"**

**DIAGRAM 4**

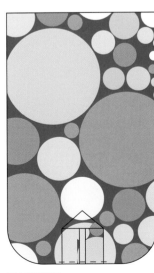

**DIAGRAM 5**

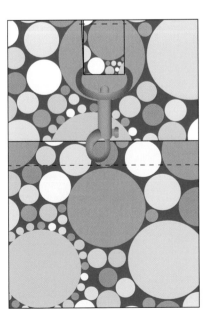

**DIAGRAM 6**

DESIGNER **JUDI KETTELER**
PHOTOGRAPHS **GREG SCHEIDEMANN**

# messenger bag

Whip up this trendy bag as a handy everyday tote or pack up your essentials for a spur-of-the-moment road trip.

*Fusible fleece attached to the back of paisley printed fabric allows this roomy shoulder bag to keep its shape.*

## materials

- 1 yard brown-and-green paisley (bag)
- 1 yard light green paisley (bag lining, strap)
- ⅓ yard brown-and-teal paisley (pocket)
- 1 yard fusible fleece
- 7" zipper
- 3—fusible, hook-and-loop ⅞" squares

Finished bag: About 15×11×3"

Quantities are for 44/45"-wide fabrics.
Measurements include ¼" seam allowances. Sew with right sides together unless otherwise stated.

**DIAGRAM 1**

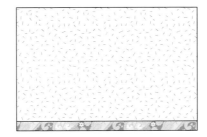

## cut fabrics

**From each brown-and-green and light green paisley, cut:**
- 1—22×19" rectangle
- 1—13×19" rectangle

**From light green paisley, cut:**
- 1—5½×41" strip

**From brown-and-teal paisley, cut:**
- 1—9×7¾" rectangle for pocket lining
- 1—9×7" rectangle for pocket front
- 1—9×2½" rectangle for pocket front

**From fusible fleece, cut:**
- 2—12×19" rectangles
- 1—2×40" strip

## assemble bag body

[1] Following manufacturer's instructions, fuse a 12×19" fleece rectangle to wrong side of one end of brown-and-green paisley 22×19" rectangle (**Diagram 1**); fuse a second fleece 12×19" rectangle to wrong side of brown-and-green paisley 13×19" rectangle.

**DIAGRAM 2**

**DIAGRAM 3**

1½"

3"

**DIAGRAM 4**

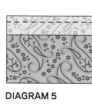

**DIAGRAM 5**

**DIAGRAM 6**

[2] Referring to **Diagram 2**, sew together brown-and-green paisley 13×19" and 22×19" rectangles to make bag front and back. Press seam open. Fold 1" of single layer of fabric to inside over fleece and sew in place.

[3] Layer bag front and back right sides together; sew together side edges (**Diagram 3**). Using tip of iron, carefully press seams open.

[4] To shape flat bottom for bag, at one corner match bottom seam line to side seam line, creating a flattened triangle (**Diagram 4**). Measuring 1½" from point of triangle, draw a 3"-long line across triangle. Sew on drawn line. Trim excess fabric. Repeat with remaining bottom corner to make bag body. Turn bag body right side out.

[5] Press bag flap side edges under ¼". Press bag flap remaining edge under ½".

## assemble bag pocket

[1] Using ⅝" seam, machine-baste together brown-and-teal paisley 9×7" rectangle and brown-and-teal paisley 9×2½" piece along long edge (**Diagram 5**). Press seam open.

[2] Center closed zipper facedown over pressed-open seam and baste in place (**Diagram 6**).

[3] Using zipper foot on machine, sew on right side of fabric ¼" from seam, clearing zipper teeth, to make pocket front. Remove basting.

[4] Partially open zipper and sew together right side of zippered pocket front to wrong side of brown-and-teal paisley 9×7¾" rectangle (pocket lining). Turn pocket to right side through partially open zipper; press.

[5] Center pocket on right side of light green paisley 22×19" rectangle, 4½" from lower edge (**Diagram 7**). Topstitch pocket to lining.

## assemble lining

[1] Referring to Assemble Bag Body, steps 2 through 4, sew together light green paisley 13×19" and 22×19" rectangles. Fold and press lining front edge under 1"; join side edges. Sew lining bottom corners to flatten bottom. Do not turn to right side.

[2] Press lining flap side edges under ¼". Press remaining edge of lining flap under ½". Topstitch folded edges.

## finish bag

[1] Insert bag lining into bag body wrong sides together. Align folded edges and seams. Topstitch bag flap and top edge of bag together, pivoting stitching at side seams (**Diagram 8**).

[2] Fold and lightly press light green paisley 5½×41" strip in half lengthwise. Open strip and press short and long edges under ¼". Layer 2×40" fusible fleece strip on one half of wrong side of light

4½"

DIAGRAM 7

DIAGRAM 8

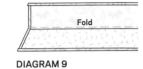

Fold

DIAGRAM 9

green paisley strip, avoiding turned-under edges (**Diagram 9**); fuse in place (do not fuse turned-under edges).

[3] Fold strip wrong sides together and topstitch folded edges.

[4] Pin strap ends to bag back just above side seams, aligning edge of strap with edge of bag. Sew handle to bag, stitching through all thicknesses.

[5] Fuse hook-and-loop squares on bag front and flap as desired.

## color option

Need a quick gift for a favorite guy? Make a masculine bag big enough to hold file folders and a lot of papers out of fashionable wool. The wool used for our bag was pre-quilted, but you can back your own wool with fusible fleece before quilting it. Then trim your quilted fabric to size, assemble the bag, and edge the flap with charcoal-brown bias-cut wool strips. To duplicate the curved-edge bag flap, draw the curve of a saucer on the lining and trim to shape.

DESIGNER **CATHY CORCELLA**
PHOTOGRAPHS **GREG SCHEIDEMANN**

# holds
## it all

Everyone will wonder where you found this high-fashion
tote and the coordinating wallet and checkbook cover.

*This bag holds enough gear to be a weekend bag; the wallet and checkbook cover*
*are the perfect accompaniments for a road trip or shopping spree.*

## materials

- 4—½-yard pieces assorted aqua-and-brown prints (bag body, lining, pocket, handle)
- 1 yard stiff interfacing (such as Timtex or Peltex)
- 1 yard lightweight fusible web
- 2½ yards ½"-diameter cording
- Magnetic snap closure
- Dressmaker's pencil

Finished bag: 14×18×6"

Quantities are for 44/45"-wide, 100% cotton fabrics. Measurements include ¼" seam allowances. Sew with right sides together unless otherwise stated.

## cut fabrics

Cut pieces in the following order.

**From assorted aqua-and-brown prints, cut:**
- 1—8×42" C rectangle
- 4—14¼×21" B rectangles
- 2—8×15" A rectangles

**From stiff interfacing, cut:**
- 1—21×28" rectangle

**From fusible web, cut:**
- 1—21×28" rectangle

## assemble pocket

Sew together A rectangles, leaving a 2" opening along one long edge (**Diagram 1**). Turn right side out through opening. Press and slip-stitch opening closed to make pocket.

## assemble bag lining

[1] Join two B rectangles along one long edge, leaving an 8" opening at center, to make a 21×28" lining rectangle (**Diagram 2**). Press seam open.

[2] Center pocket on one half of lining rectangle, 3" from upper edge (**Diagram 2**). Topstitch side and bottom edges of pocket to lining. Stitch down center of pocket to make a divided pocket.

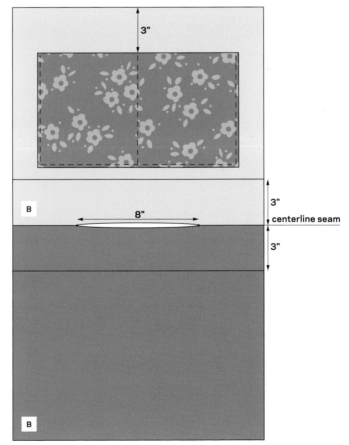

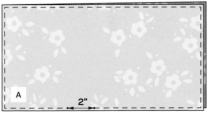

**DIAGRAM 1**

**DIAGRAM 2**

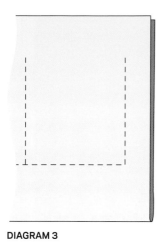

**DIAGRAM 3**

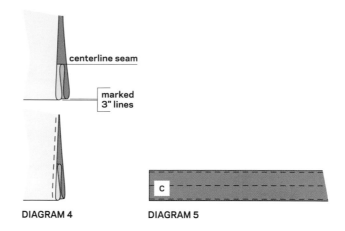

centerline seam

marked 3" lines

**DIAGRAM 4**

c

**DIAGRAM 5**

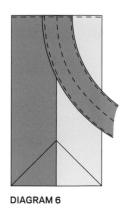

**DIAGRAM 6**

[3] Following manufacturer's instructions, attach both portions of magnetic closure to lining rectangle, centering them 2" from top and bottom edges.

[4] Use a dressmaker's pencil to mark lines 3" from centerline seam in both directions (**Diagram 2** on previous page).

[5] Fold rectangle in half, right side inside, at centerline seam (**Diagram 3**); press.

[6] Push folded edge up between lining layers, creating folds at 3" marks on both sides of centerline seam (**Diagram 4**); press. Pin sides; sew both side edges from top to bottom to make bag lining.

[7] Clip seams at folds in order to press side seams open. Do not turn bag lining right side out.

## assemble bag body

[1] Join two B rectangles along one long edge to make a 21×28" bag rectangle.

[2] Following manufacturer's instructions, press fusible-web 21×28" rectangle to wrong side of bag rectangle. Allow to cool; peel off paper backing.

[3] Press fused bag rectangle to interfacing 21×28" rectangle.

[4] Referring to Assemble Bag Lining, steps 4–7, stitch both side edges from top to bottom to make bag body. Turn bag right side out.

## assemble handle

[1] Press C rectangle in half lengthwise with wrong side inside. Open and press long raw edges to center crease with wrong side inside. Refold in half and press to make a 2×42" handle.

[2] Topstitch handle ⅛" from outer edges. Then topstitch centerline of handle to create two channels (**Diagram 5**).

[3] Cut 2½-yard piece of cording in half. Attach a safety pin to one end of one 45"-long piece and thread through a topstitched channel. Trim cording, leaving 1" at both ends of channel free of cording. Repeat with remaining cord piece and channel.

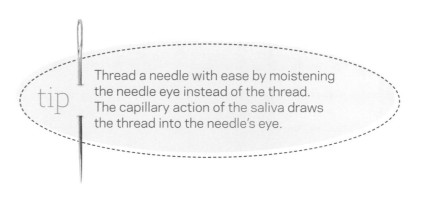

tip    Thread a needle with ease by moistening the needle eye instead of the thread. The capillary action of the saliva draws the thread into the needle's eye.

## finish bag

[1] Matching handle centerline with bag side seams, pin ends of handle to right side of bag body at top edge of each side; baste (**Diagram 6**).

[2] With right side of bag body facing out and wrong side of bag lining facing out, place bag body inside lining, matching seams and raw edges. Pin together raw edges, making sure handle is tucked between body and lining, out of the way. Using ½" seam, sew together bag and lining.

[3] Pull bag body through opening in lining to turn the Step 2 unit right side out. Press and slip-stitch opening closed. Push lining down into bag, aligning seams and corners. Press and topstitch around upper edge to finish bag.

There's no such thing as having too many tote bags . . . or too many pockets. To add more storing space to this already roomy tote, we started with the basic "Hold It All" tote and added contrasting, bias-edged pockets to both sides of the outside of the tote bag.

DESIGNER **CATHY CORCELLA**
PHOTOGRAPHS **GREG SCHEIDEMANN**

# check
# it out

Fill your Holds It All tote bag with
a fabric wallet and coordinating
checkbook cover.

*Stash your cash and your checks in this coordinated wallet and checkbook cover. Stitch a few seams, add a pleated zipper pocket, and finish off with a magnetic closure—your wallet is ready to go. The complementary checkbook cover showcases two pockets, contrasting binding, and a trendy matching button with elastic to keep it closed. Toss them both—and a host of other must-haves—in the roomy tote bag shown on page 106.*

# for the wallet

## materials

- 4—18×22" pieces (fat quarters) assorted aqua-and-brown prints (base, pockets, binding)
- ¼ yard heavyweight fusible interfacing
- ¼ yard lightweight fusible web
- ¼ yard stiff double-sided fusible interfacing (such as Fast2Fuse)
- 9"-long zipper: aqua
- Magnetic snap closure

Finished wallet: 7¾×12" (open); 7¾×4" (folded)

Measurements include ¼" seam allowances. Sew with right sides together unless otherwise stated.

## cut fabrics

Cut pieces in the following order.

**From assorted aqua-and-brown prints, cut:**
- 2—2×22" binding strips
- 1—16×7¾" D rectangle
- 2—7¾×12" E rectangles
- 1—6×7¾" C rectangle
- 1—5×7¾" B rectangle
- 1—4×7¾" A rectangle

**From fusible interfacing, cut:**
- 1—6×7¾" C rectangle
- 1—5×7¾" B rectangle
- 1—4×7¾" A rectangle

**From fusible web, cut:**
- 1—7¾×12" E rectangle

**From stiff fusible interfacing, cut:**
- 1—7¾×12" E rectangle

## assemble pockets

[1] Fuse interfacing A rectangle to wrong side of aqua-and-brown print A rectangle (see Tip, *page 114*). Fuse interfacing B rectangle to wrong side of aqua-and-brown print B rectangle, and interfacing C rectangle to wrong side of aqua-and-brown print C rectangle.

[2] With wrong side inside, fold fused A rectangle in half to make a 2×7¾" A pocket piece; press. Topstitch folded edge.

[3] With wrong side inside, fold fused B rectangle in half to make a 2½×7¾" B pocket piece; press. Topstitch folded edge.

[4] Aligning raw edges, layer A and B pocket pieces. Topstitch through center, beginning at folded edges and stopping at topstitching line on A pocket piece, to divide outer pocket and make a double-pocket piece (**Diagram 1**).

[5] With right side inside, fold fused C rectangle in half to make a 3×7¾" rectangle. Sew together 7¾" raw edges to make a C pocket piece. Turn right side out; press and topstitch folded edge.

[6] With right side inside, fold aqua-and-brown print D rectangle in half to make an 8×7¾" rectangle. Join 7¾" raw edges; press seam open. Turn right side out and press, centering seam (**Diagram 2**).

[7] Pin one folded edge of D rectangle to one side of 9"-long zipper (top zipper stop should be ⅜" from fabric edge; bottom stop extends beyond fabric edge). Sew zipper to folded edge. Pin remaining folded edge to opposite side of zipper. Open zipper and sew opposite side in place to make pocket unit (**Diagram 3**).

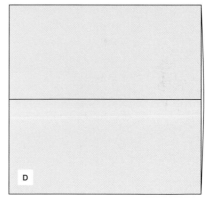

**DIAGRAM 1**

**DIAGRAM 2**

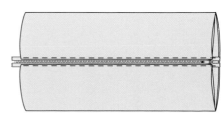

**DIAGRAM 3**

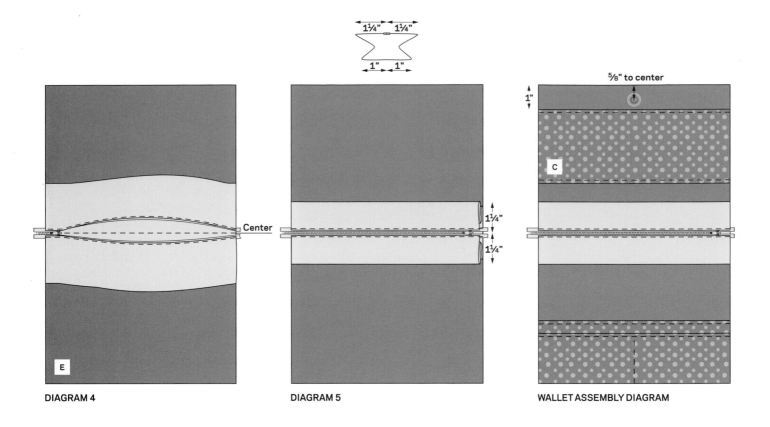

DIAGRAM 4

DIAGRAM 5

WALLET ASSEMBLY DIAGRAM

## assemble wallet

[1] Fuse stiff fusible interfacing E rectangle to wrong side of one aqua-and-brown print E rectangle to make wallet base. Peel off paper backing.

[2] Aligning center of unzipped pocket unit with center of fabric side of wallet base, straight-stitch along centerline (**Diagram 4**).

[3] Referring to **Diagram 5**, close zipper, and fold and press pocket unit accordion-style to make a $2\frac{1}{2}\times7\frac{3}{4}$" pocket. Pin pocket to wallet base at side edges.

[4] Pin C pocket piece at top end of wallet base, positioning pocket's sewn edge 1" from raw edge. Topstitch bottom edge of pocket piece to wallet base (**Wallet Assembly Diagram**).

[5] Following manufacturer's directions, attach male side of magnetic closure to wallet base, centering closure $\frac{5}{8}$" from top edge.

[6] Fuse fusible-web E rectangle to wrong side of remaining aqua-and-brown print E rectangle. Peel off paper backing and fuse

prepared rectangle to remaining side of wallet base. Turn wallet base pocket side up. Peel back the fused fabric on the bottom edge of the wallet base. Attach female side of magnetic closure to outer side of wallet, centering closure 3" from bottom edge.

[7] Using tip of iron, re-fuse loosened fabric to the wallet base.

[8] Pin double-pocket piece at bottom end of wallet base. Baste around outer edges of wallet through all layers. Trim off zipper tape extending beyond edges of wallet.

[9] Bind with aqua-and-brown print binding strips. (For details, see Better Binding, *page 206*.)

tip   Consider stitching the wallet and checkbook cover in solids that pick up just one color from the main fabric in the tote, then trim each in a complementary print.

checkbook
cover

wallet

# for the checkbook cover

## materials

- ▸ 3—18×22" pieces (fat quarters) assorted aqua-and-brown prints (cover, lining, pockets, binding)
- ▸ ¼ yard heavyweight fusible interfacing

- ▸ ¼ yard stiff double-sided fusible interfacing (such as Fast2Fuse)
- ▸ 1¼"-diameter button
- ▸ Elastic ponytail holder

Finished checkbook cover: 3½×7" (folded)

Measurements include ¼" seam allowances. Sew with right sides together unless otherwise stated.

**tip** Follow the instructions that come with your fusible web or interfacing to ensure that you are using the correct iron temperature setting and know whether to use a dry or a steam iron. Following the recommended time for pressing is critical to obtaining a secure bond between fusible material and fabric.

## cut fabrics

Cut pieces in the following order.

**From assorted aqua-and-brown prints, cut:**
▸ 2—2×22" binding strips
▸ 2—7" B squares
▸ 2—6×7" A rectangles

**From heavyweight fusible interfacing, cut:**
▸ 2—6×7" A rectangles

**From stiff fusible interfacing, cut:**
▸ 1—7" B square

## assemble pockets

[1] Following manufacturer's instructions, fuse an interfacing A rectangle to wrong side of each aqua-and-brown print A rectangle.

[2] With wrong side inside, fold a fused rectangle in half lengthwise to make a 3×7" rectangle; press folded edge. Topstitch close to fold to make a 3×7" pocket (**Diagram 1**). Repeat to make a second pocket.

## assemble checkbook cover

[1] Place stiff double-sided fusible interfacing B square on wrong side of an aqua-and-brown print B square. Following manufacturer's directions, fuse fabric to interfacing to make inside of checkbook cover. Allow to cool. Peel off paper backing.

[2] Fuse remaining aqua-and-brown print B square to remaining side of fused interfacing square to make outside of checkbook cover.

[3] Sew button to outside of checkbook cover, centering button 1¼" from top edge (**Diagram 2**). Pinch ponytail holder together; baste together, leaving a 1½" loop at one end. Pin ponytail holder to outside of cover with 1½" loop extending toward button and remaining loop extending over bottom edge. Baste loop in place.

[4] Referring to **Diagram 3**, align long raw edges of 3×7" pockets with top and bottom edges of inside of cover; baste around all edges through all layers. Trim off ponytail holder loop that extends beyond edge on right side of checkbook cover.

[5] Bind with aqua-and-brown print binding strips. (For details, see Better Binding, *page 206*.)

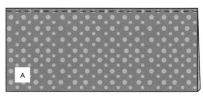

**DIAGRAM 1**

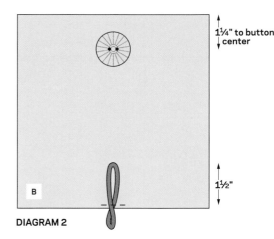

1¼" to button center

1½"

**DIAGRAM 2**

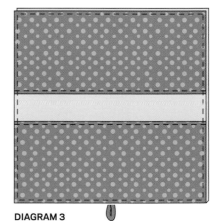

**DIAGRAM 3**

# stylefile

DESIGNER **KAREN MONTGOMERY**
PHOTOGRAPHS **GREG SCHEIDEMANN**
**AND JASON DONNELLY**

This personalized fabric portfolio sports a front pocket and zippered pouch large enough for valuable papers and files.

*An eye-catching portfolio with panache comes in handy for toting and storing papers and notes. You'll want to make several for gifts, and will enjoy selecting fabrics to suit each recipient's tastes.*

## materials

- ⅓ yard total assorted batik scraps (pocket)
- ½ yard orange batik (portfolio back, lining, pocket lining)
- ½ yard mottled deep rose (portfolio front)
- ½ yard cotton flannel (interlining)
- 20"-long zipper
- Zipper pull

Finished portfolio: 11×14"

Quantities are for 44/45"-wide fabrics.
Measurements include ½" seam allowances. Sew with right sides together unless otherwise stated.

## cut fabrics

Cut pieces in the following order.

**From assorted batik scraps, cut:**
- 7—3×17" strips

**From orange batik, cut:**
- 1—15×26" rectangle
- 1—9½×15" rectangle

**From mottled deep rose, cut:**
- 1—15×21" rectangle

**From flannel, cut:**
- 1—13×15" rectangle
- 1—11×15" rectangle
- 1—9×15" rectangle

## assemble strip-pieced pocket

[1] Cut assorted batik 3×17" strips into uneven strips. Our strips measure 1⅞" wide at one end, 2½" to 3" wide at opposite end.

[2] Sew strips together into a pieced rectangle (**Diagram 1**). Trim pieced rectangle to 9½×15" including seam allowances.

[3] Join pieced rectangle and orange batik 9½×15" rectangle along one long edge. Turn to right side. Press. Insert flannel 9×15" rectangle between folded fabric layers. Topstitch ¼" from folded edge to secure flannel. Topstitch pieced strips. Trim flannel even with fabric edges to make pocket.

## assemble portfolio

[1] Fold and press mottled deep rose 15×21" rectangle in half, making a 15×10½" rectangle. Place closed zipper inside folded mottled deep rose rectangle, allowing ends of zipper to extend beyond fabric (**Diagram 2**). Pin zipper in place, aligning one edge of zipper tape along fold.

[2] Sew ¼" to ⅜" from fold to secure zipper. Note: The closer you sew to the zipper, the less of it will show on the finished project. Be careful not to sew too close to zipper teeth so the fabric won't catch in the zipper.

[3] Open folded rectangle and fold wrong sides together to expose zipper as shown in **Diagram 3**.

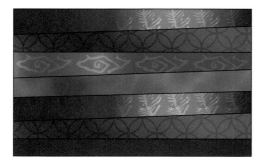

**DIAGRAM 1**

**DIAGRAM 3**

**DIAGRAM 2**

**DIAGRAM 4**

[4] Fold and press orange batik 15×26" rectangle in half to make a 15×13" rectangle. Place zipper unit inside orange batik rectangle, aligning remaining zipper tape edge along fold (**Diagram 4**). Pin in place and sew along fold as previously done. Open folded rectangle and fold it, wrong sides together, to expose zipper.

[5] Insert flannel 13×15" rectangle between orange batik layers. Topstitch ¼" from folded edge to hold flannel in place. Insert flannel 11×15" rectangle between mottled deep rose layers. Topstitch to make zippered unit (**Diagram 5**).

[6] Quilt as desired. Trim flannel even with fabric edges.

[7] Place pocket on mottled deep rose section of zippered unit, aligning bottom edges (**Diagram 6**). Baste in place by hand or machine.

[8] Fold zippered unit in half, matching raw edges; pin in place. Sew together side edge with zipper tail and across bottom of unit (**Diagram 7**). Do NOT sew side with zipper tab. (If you have a serger you can serge the side and bottom seam and trim the zipper—all in one step.)

[9] Open zipper, moving tab to tail end inside Step 8 unit. Sew or serge remaining side edge (**Diagram 8**). Trim seams, including excess zipper tape, with pinking shears, or zigzag-stitch edges to prevent fabric fraying. Turn portfolio right side out and press. Attach zipper pull.

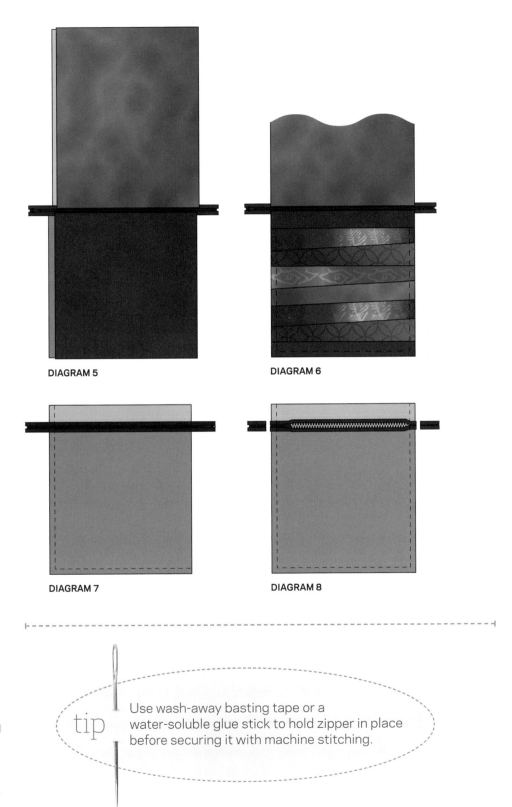

DIAGRAM 5

DIAGRAM 6

DIAGRAM 7

DIAGRAM 8

tip Use wash-away basting tape or a water-soluble glue stick to hold zipper in place before securing it with machine stitching.

143

146

129

120

# gifted touches

What better way to share your love of quilting than to give something you've made yourself? Little ones, teens, and special friends and family will cherish these handmade treasures.

Dots Nice ........................... 120
Stick to It ........................... 125
Blanket Statement ................... 129
Grand Slam ........................... 134
Tokens of Affection ................. 137
Flirty Skirts ....................... 140
Color Me Happy ....................... 143
Warm Fuzzies ......................... 146
Sweet Baby Kisses .................... 149

# dots nice

DESIGNER **TAMMY KELLY**
PHOTOGRAPHS **GREG SCHEIDEMANN**

Colorful polka dots and swirling pinwheels offer a fun visual feast in this throw-size quilt.

*Great as a gift for a teen or a recent graduate, this spirited quilt comes alive with large polka dots and colorful pinwheels. Assembly includes a two-step process of seaming to avoid setting in seams when constructing the blocks. If you haven't used this technique before, don't worry. Just follow our step-by-step directions to see how easy it is.*

## materials

- ▸ 1 yard multicolor dot (blocks, border No. 2)
- ▸ ¼ yard each pink, orange, and purple prints (blocks, border No. 1)
- ▸ ⅜ yard each mottled green, green batik, and green print (blocks)
- ▸ ⅓ yard green tone-on-tone (border No. 1)
- ▸ ¼ yard pink-and-white print (border No. 3)
- ▸ ⅜ yard mottled purple (border No. 4)

- ▸ ½ yard mottled dark pink (binding)
- ▸ 3 yards backing fabric
- ▸ 51×59" batting

Finished quilt: 45×53"
Finished block: 8" square

Quantities are for 44/45"-wide, 100% cotton fabrics. Measurements include ¼" seam allowances. Sew with right sides together unless otherwise stated.

tip

While using four assorted green prints adds visual interest to the "Dots Nice" quilt, you can simplify the design and the piecing by using just one green print throughout.

## cut fabrics

Cut pieces in the following order.

Note: To achieve the same look in your large dot border No. 2, with a row of different colored dots on each side of the quilt, cut multicolor dot border No. 2 strips ¼" away from edge of dots (to allow for seams) along the fabric width. This will result in some fabric waste. The pink dot and green dot strips will need to be pieced to the correct length. Again, allow for ¼" seam allowances when cutting strips where they will be sewn together to create a seamless row of dots.

**From multicolor dot, cut:**
- ▸ 2—1½×42" pink dot strips for border No. 2
- ▸ 2—1½×42" green dot strips for border No. 2
- ▸ 1—1½×38½" purple dot border No. 2 strip
- ▸ 1—1½×38½" orange dot border No. 2 strip
- ▸ 20—4½" squares

**From each pink, orange, and purple print, cut:**
- ▸ 4—2⅞" squares, cutting each in half diagonally for 24 triangles total (you will use 22 triangles total: 7 pink, 7 orange, and 8 purple triangles in border No. 1)
- ▸ 33—2½" squares (you will have one purple square leftover)

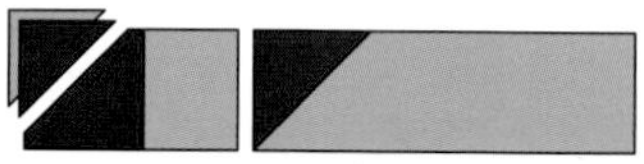

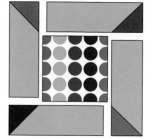

**DIAGRAM 1**

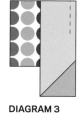

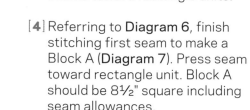

**DIAGRAM 2**

**DIAGRAM 3**

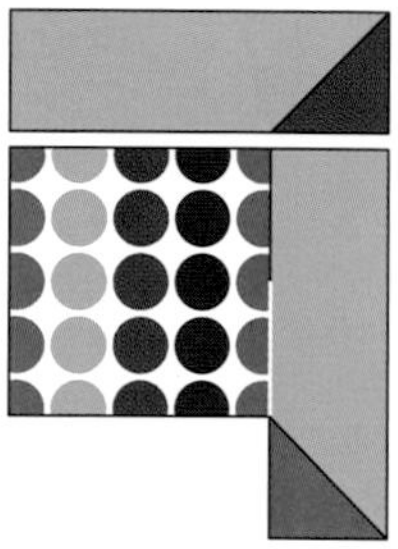

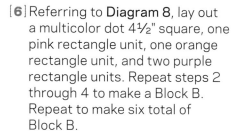

**DIAGRAM 4**

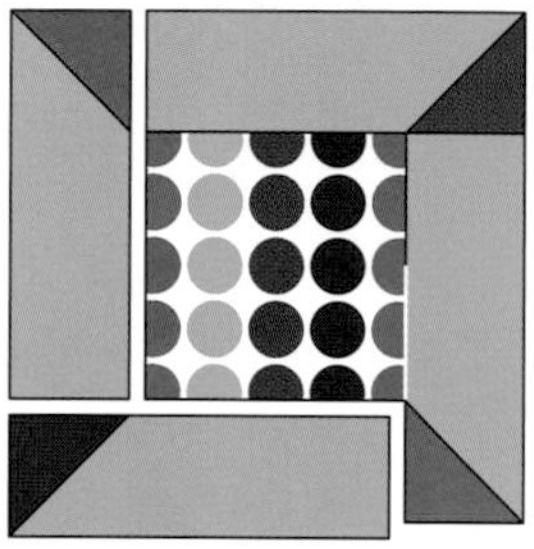

**DIAGRAM 5**

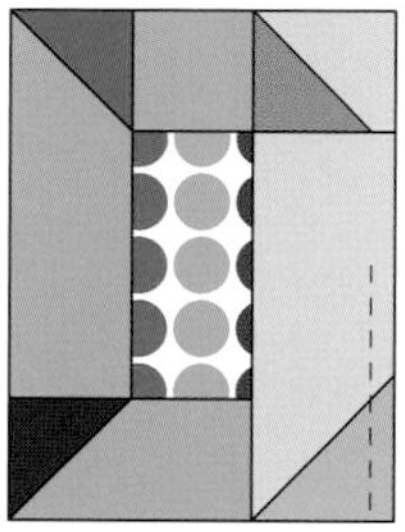

**DIAGRAM 6**

**From mottled green, green batik, and green print, cut:**
▸ 80—2½×6½" rectangles

**From green tone-on-tone, cut:**
▸ 18—2½×6½" rectangles
▸ 11—2⅞" squares, cutting each in half diagonally for 22 triangles total

**From pink-and-white print, cut:**
▸ 5—1½×42" strips for border No. 3

**From mottled purple, cut:**
▸ 5—2¾×42" strips for border No. 4

**From mottled dark pink, cut:**
▸ 5—2½×42" binding strips

## assemble units

[1] Use a pencil to mark a diagonal line on wrong side of each pink, orange, and purple print 2½" square. (Set aside six squares of each color to use in border No. 1.)

[2] Align a marked pink square with one end of a mottled green, green batik, or green print 2½×6½" rectangle (**Diagram 1**; note direction of drawn line). Sew on marked line. Trim excess

fabric, leaving ¼" seam allowance. Press open attached triangle to make a pink rectangle unit. Repeat to make 27 pink rectangle units total.

[3] Using orange and purple 2½" squares and remaining mottled green, green batik, and green print 2½×6½" rectangles, repeat Step 2 to make 27 orange rectangle units and 26 purple rectangle units total.

## assemble blocks

[1] Referring to **Diagram 2**, lay out a multicolor dot 4½" square, one purple rectangle unit, one pink rectangle unit, and two orange rectangle units.

[2] Join 4½" square and first rectangle unit sewing only half of the seam (**Diagram 3**). Finger-press seam toward rectangle unit.

[3] Add next rectangle unit counterclockwise to the first rectangle unit (**Diagram 4**).

Add remaining rectangle units in sequence (**Diagram 5**). Press all seams toward rectangle units.

[4] Referring to **Diagram 6**, finish stitching first seam to make a Block A (**Diagram 7**). Press seam toward rectangle unit. Block A should be 8½" square including seam allowances.

[5] Repeat steps 1 through 4 to make seven total of Block A.

[6] Referring to **Diagram 8**, lay out a multicolor dot 4½" square, one pink rectangle unit, one orange rectangle unit, and two purple rectangle units. Repeat steps 2 through 4 to make a Block B. Repeat to make six total of Block B.

[7] Referring to **Diagram 9**, lay out a multicolor dot 4½" square, one orange rectangle unit, one purple rectangle unit, and two pink rectangle units. Repeat steps 2 through 4 to make a Block C. Repeat to make seven total of Block C.

## assemble quilt center

[1] Referring to **Quilt Assembly Diagram**, lay out blocks A, B, and C in five horizontal rows.

[2] Sew together blocks in each row. Press seams in one direction, alternating direction with each row.

[3] Join rows to make quilt center. Press seams in one direction. Quilt center should be 32½×40½" including seam allowances.

## assemble and add border no. 1

[1] Sew together a pink triangle and a green tone-on-tone triangle to make a pink triangle-square (**Diagram 10**). Press seam

toward green triangle. Repeat to make seven pink triangle-squares total.

[2] Repeat Step 1 using orange and purple triangles and remaining green tone-on-tone triangles to make seven orange triangle-squares and eight purple triangle-squares total.

[3] Align a marked pink print 2½" square with one end of a green tone-on-tone 2½×6½" rectangle. Sew, trim, and press as in Assemble Units, Step 2, to make a pink border unit. Repeat to make six pink border units total. Repeat with marked orange print and purple print 2½" squares and green tone-on-tone 2½×6½" rectangles to make six orange border units and six purple border units total.

[4] Referring to **Quilt Assembly Diagram** for color placement, sew together five triangle-squares and five border units to make a long border No. 1 strip. Long border No. 1 strip should be 2½×40½" including seam allowances. Repeat to make a second long border No. 1 strip.

[5] Sew together six triangle-squares and four border units to make a short border No. 1 strip (**Quilt Assembly Diagram**). Short border No. 1 strip should be 2½×36½" including seam allowances. Repeat to make a second short border No. 1 strip.

[6] Add long border No. 1 strips to long edges of quilt center. Add short border No. 1 strips to remaining edges. Press all seams toward border.

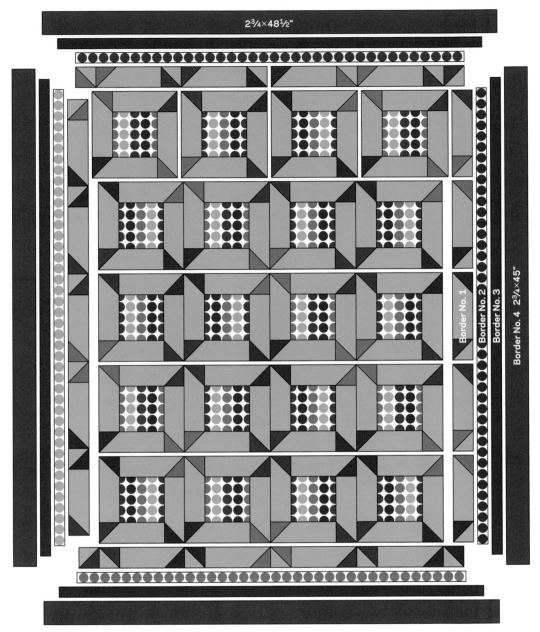

2¾×48½"

Border No. 1
Border No. 2
Border No. 3
Border No. 4  2¾×45"

**QUILT ASSEMBLY DIAGRAM**

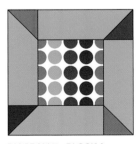

**DIAGRAM 7 – BLOCK A**

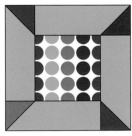

**DIAGRAM 8 – BLOCK B**

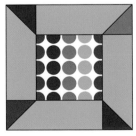

**DIAGRAM 9 – BLOCK C**

**DIAGRAM 10**

## assemble and add border no. 2

[1] Cut and piece pink and green multicolor dot 1½×42" strips to make:
- 1—1½×44½" pink dot border No. 2 strip
- 1—1½×44½" green dot border No. 2 strip

[2] Sew pink dot and green dot border No. 2 strips to long edges of quilt center. Add purple dot and orange dot 1½×38½" border No. 2 strips to remaining edges. Press all seams toward border No. 2.

## assemble and add border no. 3 and no. 4

[1] Cut and piece pink-and-white print 1½×42" strips to make the following:
- 2—1½×46½" border No. 3 strips
- 2—1½×40½" border No. 3 strips

[2] Sew long border No. 3 strips to long edges of quilt center. Sew short border No. 3 strips to remaining edges. Press all seams toward border No. 3.

[3] Cut and piece mottled purple 2¾×42" strips to make:
- 2—2¾×48½" border No. 4 strips
- 2—2¾×45" border No. 4 strips

[4] Sew long border No. 4 strips to long edges of quilt center. Sew short border No. 4 strips to remaining edges to complete quilt top. Press all seams toward border No. 4.

## color option

Sometimes simple is best. Follow our lead and use the basic elements of "Dots Nice"–squares and rectangles–to create this cozy throw using a more traditional color scheme. To make a quilt like this, cut red prints into 4½" squares and medium and dark blue prints into 2½×4½" rectangles. Join the contrasting blue prints in pairs to make 4½" squares. Sew the squares together in an alternating pattern. Top it off with a paisley pattern stitched across the quilt top and a dark blue print binding along the edges. QUILTMAKERS **MARY PEPPER AND KATHLEEN WILLIAMS**

## finish quilt

[1] Layer quilt top, batting, and backing; baste. (For details, see Quilt It, *page 197.*)

[2] Quilt as desired. Machine-quilter Linda DeVries stitched a double-loop vine and crescent motifs in green thread across the quilt center. Vining loops in a variegated thread accent the middle and outer borders.

[3] Bind with mottled dark pink binding strips. (For details, see Better Binding, *page 206.*)

# stick to it

DESIGNER **JEAN BAILEY OF WILDCAT STUDIOS**
PHOTOGRAPHS **CAMERON SADEGHPOUR AND SCOTT LITTLE**

Frame your favorite subject with a fabric print that suits his or her style, then showcase them on the fridge.

strip-insertion block

diamond block

double-border block

courthouse steps block

*Choose your favorite block from the four designs here—Courthouse Steps, Strip-Insertion, Double-Border, or Diamond block—for an interesting way to highlight school photos or a favorite snapshot. These quick-to-make frames are great for giving to friends and relatives, and the muslin backing is a nice place to write a special message to the recipient.*

## materials for one frame

*(Refer to Select Materials and specific block instructions for more information.)*

- 1¾×2½" to 2×3" photograph
- Fabric scraps in assorted colors (block)
- 8×12" rectangle muslin (backing)
- 8" square lightweight cotton batting
- 8" square stiff interfacing
- 2×5" flat magnet
- Fine-point permanent marking pen

Finished frames: 6×6¼" (Courthouse Steps); 5×7" (Double-Border and Strip-Insertion); 6½" square (Diamond)

Measurements include a ¼" seam allowance. Sew with right sides together unless otherwise stated.

## cut and assemble courthouse steps block

**From print No. 1, cut:**
- 1—2½×3¾" rectangle for block center

**From print No. 2, cut:**
- 2—1½×3¾" rectangles for positions 1 and 2

**From print No. 3, cut:**
- 2—1¾×4½" rectangles for positions 3 and 4

**From print No. 4, cut:**
- 2—1¼×6¼" rectangles for positions 5 and 6

**From photograph, cut:**
- 1—1¾×2½" rectangle

**DIAGRAM 1**

Sew position 1 and 2 rectangles to long edges of the 2½×3¾" block center. Press seams toward position 1 and 2 rectangles. Referring to **Diagram 1**, continue adding rectangles in numerical order to make a Courthouse Steps block. Always press seams away from the center. The block should be 6×6¼" including seam allowances. Proceed to Finish Frame, *page 128.*

## cut and assemble double-border block

**From print No. 1, cut:**
- 1—2½×3½" rectangle for block center

**From print No. 2, cut:**
- 2—1¼×5" inner border strips
- 2—1¼×2½" inner border strips

**From print No. 3, cut:**
- 2—1×7" outer border strips
- 2—1½×4" outer border strips

**From photograph, cut:**
- 1—1¾×2½" rectangle

Sew short inner border strips to short edges of the block center. Sew long inner border strips to remaining edges of block center. Press all seams toward inner border. Repeat to add outer border strips to block center to make the double-border block. The block should be 5×7" including seam allowances. Proceed to Finish Frame, *page 128.*

## cut and assemble strip-insertion block

**From print No. 1, cut:**
- 1—6×8" rectangle

**From print No. 2, cut:**
- 2—1×8" strips

**From photograph, cut:**
- 1—1¾×2½" rectangle

tip Don't limit yourself to the fridge or a file cabinet. For fun, add these frames to a magnetic memo board or the inside of a metal entry door to your house.

courthouse steps block

## cut and assemble diamond block

Pattern can be found on *Pattern Sheet 2*. To make a template of the pattern, see "What are Templates?" on *page 201*.

**From print No. 1, cut:**
▸ 1 of Diamond Pattern

**From print No. 2, cut:**
▸ 4—2½×7" strips
▸ 2—1¼×6½" strips

**From print No. 3, cut:**
▸ 2—1×6½" strips

**From photograph, cut:**
▸ 1—1¾×2½" rectangle

[1] Join print No. 2—2½×7" strips to opposite sides of print No. 1 diamond. Trim strip edges even with diamond edges (**Diagram 5**). Add 2½×7" strips to remaining edges to make a bordered diamond.

[2] Trim bordered diamond to 4×6½" including seam allowances (**Diagram 6**).

[3] Join print No. 3—1×6½" strips to the side edges of the bordered diamond. Join print No. 2—1¼×6½" strips to side edges to make the diamond block (**Diagram 7**). Press all seams toward outer edges. The block should be 6½" square including seam allowances. Proceed to Finish Frame, *page 128*.

[1] Place an acrylic ruler at a slight angle on one corner of the print No. 1—6×8" rectangle (**Diagram 2**). Cut across corner; save the resulting corner triangle.

[2] Join a print No. 2—1×8" strip to the cut edge of the rectangle (**Diagram 3**). Sew the corner triangle to the other edge of the

print No. 2 strip (**Diagram 4**). Press all seams toward the print No. 2 strip.

[3] Repeat steps 1 and 2 to insert remaining print No. 2 strip on opposite corner.

[4] Trim the pieced rectangle to 5×7", including seam allowances, to complete the strip-insertion block. Proceed to Finish Frame, *page 128*.

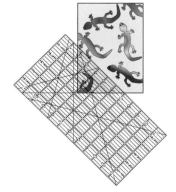

**DIAGRAM 2**

**DIAGRAM 3**

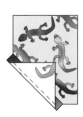

**DIAGRAM 4**

**DIAGRAM 5**

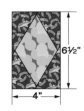

6½"

4"

**DIAGRAM 6**

**DIAGRAM 7**

## finish frame

[1] Layer a batting 8" square on a stiff interfacing 8" square, then center the pieced block on top.

[2] Quilt as desired. Jean machine-quilted in the ditch of all seams. On some of her featured frames, she also stipple-quilted the block background, used decorative machine stitches to add more texture, or quilted around motifs in the fabric prints.

[3] Place photograph in block center; use a small piece of double-stick tape to hold photo in place. Using a wide (4 mm) and long (2 mm) zigzag, machine-stitch around photograph. Allow the zigzag to fall about half on and half off the edge. Trim batting and interfacing even with block edges.

[4] Fold under 2½" on one short end of the muslin 8×12" backing rectangle; topstitch in place close to the raw edge to make the magnet pocket (**Diagram 8**). With raw edge of pocket facing up, place quilted block right side up atop muslin backing rectangle; the magnet pocket should align with the top of the block. Pin muslin backing to block and trim even with block edges.

[5] Set up your sewing machine for a 4-mm-wide, 1-mm-long zigzag stitch. Starting at the upper left corner of the layered block, stitch clockwise around all edges; when you reach the left-hand side of the magnet pocket, slip magnet into pocket (**Diagram 9**). Finish stitching to the upper edge to make the frame.

## color option

Show off your sweet new addition in style by adapting the fabric frame into a baby announcement. A fine-line fabric marking pen and light-color fabrics surrounding the photo make it easy to personalize each frame with all the pertinent details. And because the frame is magnetic, it's immediately ready for friends and family to display.

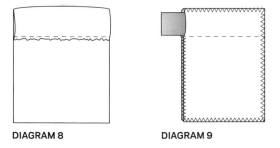

**DIAGRAM 8**        **DIAGRAM 9**

Whether from concerts, sports teams, or other events, create a keepsake by turning favorite T-shirts into a memory-filled quilt.

# blanket
## statement

DESIGNERS **ELIZABETH TISINGER**
AND **HANNA PIEPEL**
PHOTOGRAPHS **CAMERON
SADEGHPOUR**

*Because T-shirt logo size can vary widely, it can be tough to fit them into traditional quilt patterns. This versatile T-shirt quilt uses both 14"- and 7"-wide logo rectangles, giving you the flexibility to show off a wide selection of shirts.*

## materials

- 15 or more T-shirts with logos
- 6 or more solid-color plain T-shirts
- ⅝ yard solid black (binding)
- 4 yards backing fabric
- 70×81" batting
- 10 yards fusible tricot interfacing

Finished quilt: 64×75"

Quantities are for 44/45"-wide, 100% cotton fabrics. Measurements include a ½" seam allowance. Sew with right sides together unless otherwise stated.

## prepare t-shirts

Some people think sewing stretchy fabrics is tough, but we've made it easy by giving you the secret— fusible tricot interfacing. Without adding a lot of bulk, this lightweight knit interfacing prevents T-shirt knit from stretching out of shape while you're cutting and sewing. Look for interfacing brand names such as So Sheer or Fusi-Knit.

The greatest stretch of most T-shirts goes around the body (crosswise). To stabilize the shirts, place the interfacing so its stretch goes opposite the T-shirt's stretchiest direction. (Ususally, this means putting the interfacing's greatest stretch running lengthwise.)

[1] Cut each T-shirt up the sides and across the top to separate the front and back; remove the sleeves.

[2] Cut large rectangles of fusible tricot interfacing to cover the fronts and backs of the T-shirts you're using.

[3] Place each T-shirt front or back wrong side up on your work surface. With greatest stretch going in opposite directions, place fusible-web rectangles on T-shirts, fusible side down. Following the manufacturer's instructions, fuse in place; let cool.

[4] Divide prepared T-shirts with logos into two piles—a narrow pile (logos that will fit best in a 6"-wide-finished row) and a wide pile (logos that will fit better in a 13"-wide-finished row). (Depending on the size of T-shirts you're using, you may wish to adapt the width of your rows to better accommodate the logos.)

## give yourself a break!

A quilt made of all T-shirts can be heavy and awkward to machine-quilt, so consider hiring a long-arm quilting professional to do the job. Just like the clothes it's made from, your quilt will probably get a lot of wear and tear, so have it more densely quilted to help it retain its shape after washing. Choose a polyester or cotton/poly-blend batting to avoid adding extra weight.

tip

Making a T-shirt quilt as a graduation gift? Include a few light-color T-shirts in your quilt where friends and family can add their autographs and well-wishes using a fabric marker.

## cut logo rectangles

**From *each* interfaced logo shirt in wide pile, cut:**
▸ 1—14"-wide rectangle, centering logo across width and cutting at least 1" above and below logo where possible

**From *each* interfaced logo shirt in narrow pile, cut:**
▸ 1—7"-wide rectangle, centering logo across width and cutting at least 1" above and below logo where possible

## cut remaining fabrics

The quilt top will be assembled in seven vertical rows—four narrow and three wide (**Quilt Assembly Diagram**). To cut the solid-color rectangles you'll need to fill in the spaces between logo rectangles, refer to the following:

**Wide rows:** Add heights of 14"-wide logo rectangles (subtracting 1" from each height for seam allowances). Subtract this amount from 250" to get an estimated total amount needed.

**Narrow rows:** Add heights of 7"-wide logo rectangles (subtracting 1" from each height for seam allowances). Subtract this amount from 350" to get an estimated total amount needed.

**From interfaced solid-color plain shirts and scraps of remaining logo shirts, cut:**
▸ Enough 14"-wide rectangles in heights varying from 2" to 6" to equal amount determined above
▸ Enough 7"-wide rectangles in heights varying from 2" to 20" to equal amount determined above

**From solid black, cut:**
▸ 8—2½×42" binding strips

## assemble quilt top

[1] Referring to **Quilt Assembly Diagram**, lay out all pieces in seven vertical rows, distributing logo rectangles evenly throughout the rows.

**QUILT ASSEMBLY DIAGRAM**

[2] Join pieces in each row using a ½" seam allowance to make four narrow rows and three wide rows. Press all seams open. If necessary, trim each row to 75" long.

[3] Join all rows to complete quilt top. Press seams open.

## finish quilt

[1] Layer quilt top, batting, and backing; baste. (For details, see Quilt It, *page 197*.)

[2] Quilt as desired. Using black thread, machine-quilter Nancy Sharr stitched an allover stipple over the quilt top.

[3] Bind with solid black binding strips. (For details, see Better Binding, *page 206*.)

## color option

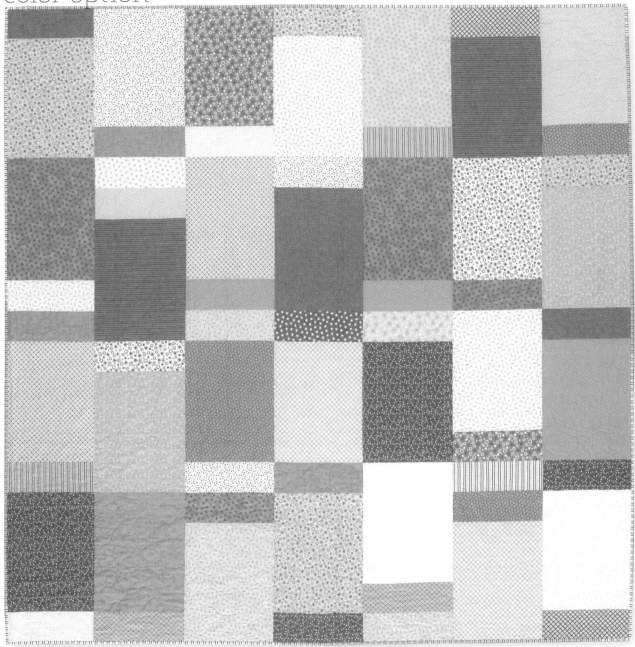

If you're not interested in making quilts from T-shirts, try the fat-quarter-friendly variation of "Blanket Statement" above, which uses cotton prints in pink. To make it even easier, we eliminated the narrow rows.

For the 91½×91" quilt, cut 30 fat quarters into 28—13½×17½" rectangles and 35—13½×5" rectangles. Mix and match rectangles in seven vertical rows of five small rectangles and four large rectangles each, then join with ¼" seams.

PHOTOGRAPH **CRAIG ANDERSON**

# grand slam

Use leftover scraps, cut strips from Grandpa's old shirts, or chop up thrift store duds to make this cozy chill chaser.

DESIGNERS **ELISSA AND HEATHER WILMS**
PHOTOGRAPHS **GREG SCHEIDEMANN AND SCOTT LITTLE**

*For the chunky Rail Fence blocks, plaid and stripe homespuns and flannels mix for a patchy look that's perfect for guys (and girls) of all ages. To pull the scrappy blocks together, the same green plaid is repeated in every block.*

## materials

- 3¾ yards total assorted plaids and stripes (blocks)
- 2⅝ yards green plaid (blocks, binding)
- 5⅛ yards backing fabric
- 67×91" batting

Finished quilt: 60½×84½"
Finished block: 6" square

Quantities are for 44/45"-wide, 100% cotton fabrics. Measurements include a ¼" seam allowance. Sew with right sides together unless otherwise stated.

**tip** — Flannels and homespuns can shrink more than other cottons. We recommend prewashing your fabrics for this quilt, especially if you're combining new fabrics with recycled scraps.

## cut fabrics

To make the best use of your fabrics, cut pieces in the following order.

**From assorted plaids and stripes, cut:**
- 48—2½×42" strips

**From green plaid, cut:**
- 24—2½×42" strips
- 8—2½×42" binding strips

## assemble blocks

[1] Sew an assorted plaid or stripe 2½×42" strip to each long edge of a green plaid 2½×42" strip to make a strip set (**Strip Set Diagram**). Press seams toward outer strips. Repeat to make 24 strip sets total.

[2] Cut strip sets into 6½"-wide segments to make 140 Rail Fence blocks total.

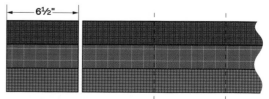

6½"

**STRIP SET DIAGRAM**

## assemble quilt top

[1] Referring to photograph, lay out blocks in 14 rows, turning every other block a quarter turn. Join blocks in each row. Press seams in one direction, alternating direction with each row.

[2] Sew together rows to complete quilt top. Press seams in one direction.

## finish quilt

[1] Layer quilt top, batting, and backing; baste. (For details, see Quilt It, *page 197*.)

[2] Quilt as desired. Heather machine-quilted an allover leaf pattern across the quilt top.

[3] Bind with green plaid binding strips. (For details, see Better Binding, *page 206*.)

# tokens
## of affection

PHOTOGRAPH
**PERRY STRUSE**

Cheerful pieced and appliquéd friendship quilts express
a quilter's sentiments better than a greeting card.

*Use bright batik scraps to make these mini thinking-of-you keepsake quilts. The piecing is quick, and machine appliqué accents the flowers. Covered cording in a contrasting fabric sets off the bound edges.*

## materials for two quilts

- 18×22" piece (fat quarter) blue-green batik (appliqué foundation, binding)
- 9×22" piece (fat eighth) green batik (appliqué foundation)
- Scraps of bright pink, yellow, and olive green batiks (flower and leaf appliqués)
- ⅛ yard blue batik (flower appliqués, border, covered cording)
- ⅛ yard pink batik (border, covered cording)
- ⅛ yard light green batik (border)
- 9×22" piece (fat eighth) orange batik (binding)

- ⅜ yard backing fabric
- 2—13" squares batting
- 2⅓ yards ¹⁄₁₆"-diameter cording
- Machine embroidery thread: bright pink, yellow, olive green, teal, orange, gold
- Lightweight fusible web

Finished quilts: 9¼" square

Quantities are for 44/45"-wide, 100% cotton fabrics. Measurements include a ¼" seam allowance. Sew with right sides together unless otherwise stated.

## cut fabrics

Cut pieces in the following order. Patterns can be found on *Pattern Sheet 2*. To use fusible web for appliquéing, complete the following steps.

[1] Lay fusible web, paper side up, over patterns. Use a pencil to trace each pattern the number of times indicated in cutting instructions, leaving ½" between tracings. Cut out each fusible-web shape roughly ¼" outside traced lines.

[2] Following manufacturer's instructions, press fusible-web shapes onto backs of designated fabrics; let cool.

[3] Cut out fabric shapes on drawn lines. Peel off paper backings.

**From blue-green batik, cut:**
- 2—2½×22" binding strips
- 1—7" square

**From green batik, cut:**
- 1—7" square

**From bright pink batik scraps, cut:**
- 1 *each* of patterns F, H, and J

**From yellow batik scraps, cut:**
- 1 *each* of patterns E, G, and I

**From olive green batik scraps, cut:**
- 1 *each* of patterns A, B, C, D, K, L, M, and N
- 3 of Pattern O

**From blue batik, cut:**
- 1—¾×42" strip for covered cording
- 12—1¾" squares
- 9 *each* of patterns P and P reversed

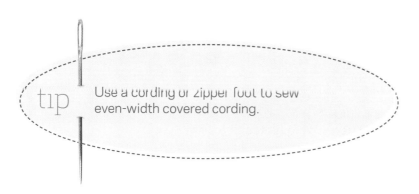

tip  Use a cording or zipper foot to sew even-width covered cording.

QUILT ASSEMBLY DIAGRAM

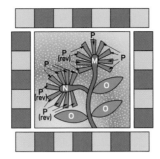

QUILT ASSEMBLY DIAGRAM

**From pink batik, cut:**
- 1—¾×42" strip for covered cording
- 12—1¾" squares

**From light green batik, cut:**
- 24—1¾" squares

**From orange batik, cut:**
- 2—2½×22" binding strips

**From cording, cut:**
- 2—42" pieces

## appliqué blocks

[1] Referring to **Quilt Assembly Diagrams**, arrange designated appliqué pieces for each block atop blue-green batik and green batik 7" squares. Fuse pieces in place.

[2] Using thread that matches the appliqués and working from bottom layer to top, straight-stitch around each appliqué piece, 1/16" from the edges. Using contrasting machine-embroidery threads and a free-motion zigzag, stitch around flower appliqués and embellish flower centers to make a bright pink appliquéd block and a blue appliquéd block.

[3] With design centered, trim each appliquéd block to measure 6¾" square including seam allowances.

## add borders

[1] Referring to **Quilt Assembly Diagram**, lay out three pink batik 1¾" squares and two light green batik 1¾" squares in a row, alternating colors. Join pieces to make a short border unit. Press seams in one direction. Repeat to make a second short border unit.

[2] Lay out four light green batik 1¾" squares and three pink batik 1¾" squares in a row, alternating colors. Sew together to make a long border unit. Press seams in one direction. Repeat to make a second long border unit.

[3] Sew short border units to opposite edges of bright pink appliquéd block. Join long border units to remaining edges to complete pink quilt top. Press seams toward border.

[4] Repeat steps 1 through 3 with blue batik 1¾" squares, the remaining light green batik 1¾" squares, and blue appliquéd block to complete blue quilt top.

## finish quilts

[1] Layer each quilt top, batting, and backing; baste. (For details, see Quilt It, *page 197.*)

[2] Quilt as desired. Trim batting and backing even with each quilt top.

[3] Cover one cording piece with blue batik ¾×42" strip. Cut covered cording into four 9¼" lengths. Aligning raw edges and using a machine cording foot, stitch a length of covered cording to each edge of pink quilt.

[4] Repeat Step 3 with remaining cording piece and pink batik ¾×42" strip to make covered cording and attach it to blue quilt.

[5] Bind pink quilt with orange batik binding strips. Bind blue quilt with blue-green batik binding strips. (For details, see Better Binding, *page 206.*)

# flirty skirts

DESIGNER **TANYA WHELAN**
PHOTOGRAPHS **GREG SCHEIDEMANN**

Stitch up some bouncy little skirts for kids or grandkids in just a few hours—no pattern needed.

*Your favorite little girl will love to twirl around in one of these multilayered skirts. To make it, simply cut straight strips from coordinating fabrics, gather at the dropped waist and hip, and add elastic in a fold-over casing. Hem and trim each layer as you like.*

## materials

**For sizes 3/4, 5/6, and 7/8:**
▸ ½ yard green floral
▸ ½ yard green polka dot

**For size 9/10:**
▸ ¾ yard pink floral
▸ ¾ yard pink polka dot

**All sizes:**
▸ ¾"-wide elastic

Finished skirts:
**Size 3/4:**
length: 10⅛"
width at hem: 48"

**Size 5/6:**
length: 13⅛"
width at hem: 49"
**Size 7/8:**
length: 16⅛"
width at hem: 50"
**Size 9/10:**
length: 19⅛"
width at hem: 51"

Quantities are for 44/45"-wide, 100% cotton fabrics. Measurements include ¼" seam allowances. Sew with right sides together unless otherwise stated.

tip To add more flair to your flirty skirt, edgestitch lace or ruffle trim to the hem of each layer.

**DIAGRAM 1**

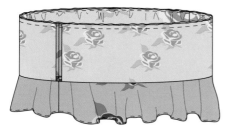

**DIAGRAM 2**

**DIAGRAM 3**

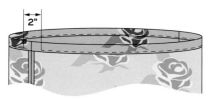

**DIAGRAM 4**

## cut fabrics

Cut pieces in the following order.

### size 3/4

**From green floral, cut:**
- 2—6¼×24½" rectangles for upper ruffle
- 2—5×13" rectangles for upper band

**From green polka dot, cut:**
- 2—4¾×24½" rectangles for lower ruffle
- 2—3¼×13" rectangles for lower band

### size 5/6

**From green floral, cut:**
- 2—7¼×25" rectangles for upper ruffle
- 2—6×13½" rectangles for upper band

**From green polka dot, cut:**
- 2—5¾×25" rectangles for lower ruffle
- 2—4¼×13½" rectangles for lower band

### size 7/8

**From green floral, cut:**
- 2—8¼×25½" rectangles for upper ruffle
- 2—7×14" rectangles for upper band

**From green polka dot, cut:**
- 2—6¾×25½" rectangles for lower ruffle
- 2—5¼×14" rectangles for lower band

### size 9/10

**From pink floral, cut:**
- 2—9¼×26" rectangles for upper ruffle
- 2—8×14½" rectangles for upper band

**From pink polka dot, cut:**
- 2—7¾×26" rectangles for lower ruffle
- 2—6¼×14½" rectangles for lower band

## assemble skirt

[1] Sew together upper band rectangles along short edges to make a tube (Diagram 1).

[2] Join upper ruffle rectangles along short edges to make a ruffle tube. Turn under ¼" on one long edge of ruffle tube; press. Turn under a second time ¼"; press. Sew through all layers close to first folded edge to hem.

[3] With a long machine basting stitch, sew ¼" from long raw edge of ruffle tube. Pull up threads to gather edge.

[4] With raw edges aligned and right sides together, match seams of gathered ruffle with bottom edge of upper band; adjust ruffle to fit band. Pin and stitch to make upper skirt unit (Diagram 2). Press seam allowance toward upper band.

[5] Repeat steps 1 through 4 using lower band rectangles and lower ruffle rectangles to make lower skirt unit.

[6] With raw edges aligned, match seams of right side lower band with wrong side of upper ruffle where upper band and upper ruffle are joined; sew through all layers (Diagram 3).

[7] Turn under top edge of skirt ½"; press. Turn under a second time 1⅛"; press. Sew through all layers close to the first folded edge, leaving a 2" opening for inserting elastic (Diagram 4).

[8] Insert elastic and adjust to fit. Sew ends of elastic together. Sew opening shut.

# color me
# happy

DESIGNER **LINDA LUM DEBONO**
PHOTOGRAPHS **GREG SCHEIDEMANN**

Make this merry crayon roll for your favorite little one.
It's a great gift to give for a birthday or as a holiday surprise.

*The small size of this quilted crayon holder makes it perfect for tucking into a backpack or purse, keeping it at the ready for creating artwork on the go. It has space for holding 12 favorite colors and neatly rolls up when not in use.*

## materials

- 18×22" piece (fat quarter) multicolor floral (cover, pocket)
- 9×22" piece (fat eighth) green stripe (lining)
- ⅛ yard blue polka dot (tie, binding)
- 6½×12½" batting
- Water- or air-soluble marking pen

Finished crayon roll: 6½×12½"

Quantities are for 44/45"-wide, 100% cotton fabrics. Measurements include ¼" seam allowances. Sew with right sides together unless otherwise stated.

## cut fabrics

Cut pieces in the following order.

**From multicolor floral, cut:**
- 1—7½×12½" pocket rectangle
- 1—6½×12½" cover rectangle

**From green stripe, cut:**
- 1—6½×12½" lining rectangle

**From blue polka dot, cut:**
- 1—2½×42" binding strip
- 1—1½×42" strip for tie

## assemble crayon roll

[1] Wrong side inside, fold and press multicolor floral 7½×12½" rectangle in half lengthwise to make a 3¾×12½" pocket rectangle.

[2] Layer multicolor floral 6½×12½" cover rectangle wrong side up, 6½×12½" batting rectangle, green stripe 6½×12½" lining rectangle right side up, and pocket rectangle (**Diagram 1**). Pin layers together.

[3] Set up your machine with a walking (even-feed) foot and a straight-stitch throat plate. Mark stitching lines with a

water- or air-soluble marking pen. Quilt layered roll with straight-stitch lines beginning 1¼" from a short edge (**Diagram 2**). Continue quilting straight lines at 1"-wide intervals across surface of roll. Leave 1¼" unquilted along opposite short edge.

[4] Wrong side inside, fold and press blue polka dot 1½×42" strip in half lengthwise. Open strip and press long edges to center fold line. Topstitch ⅛" from folded edges to make tie. Knot each end of tie and trim excess fabric at an angle to prevent raveling.

[5] Fold tie in half. Pin center of tie to lining side of roll, aligning tie with folded top edge of pocket, to complete roll (**Diagram 3**).

[6] Bind with blue polka dot binding strip, keeping tie ends free from stitching. (For details, see Better Binding, page *206*.) Top-stitch edge of binding.

## color option

Little girls will be tickled pink to receive a crayon roll made in their favorite color fabric. For little guys, choose a novelty fabric—cowboys, fire trucks, or whimsical critters—that reflects their current interest. For an instant hit, couple the crayon roll with a pint-size tablet of drawing paper.

DIAGRAM 1

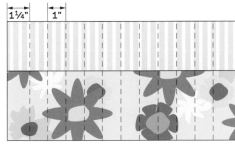

DIAGRAM 2

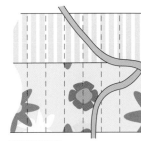

DIAGRAM 3

# warm fuzzies

You'll love this fluffy scarf so much that you'll want to make one for each of your friends.

DESIGNER **JENNY WILDING CARDON**
PHOTOGRAPHS **GREG SCHEIDEMANN**

*This oh-so-soft scarf is much easier than it looks. Once you've stitched the rows of colored rectangles together, just sandwich two layers of pieced rows together with batting, cut the curvy edges using the pattern, and add a simple binding.*

## materials

- ¼ yard each solid light blue, yellow, lavender, light green, and pink knit-back fleece
- 6¼×45½" rectangle batting
- Quilt-basting spray or fabric glue stick
- Air-soluble marking pen
- Template plastic

Finished scarf: 6¼×45½"

Quantities are for 58/59"-wide, 100% polyester, knit-back fleece. Measurements include ¼" seam allowances. Sew with right sides together unless otherwise stated.

## cut fabrics

Cut pieces in the following order. Pattern can be found on *Pattern Sheet 2*. To make and use template for cutting pattern, see "What Are Templates?" on *page 201*.

**From each solid light blue, yellow, lavender, light green, and pink knit-back fleece, cut:**
- 6—3½×6¼" rectangles (30 rectangles total)

**From remaining solid light blue knit-back fleece, cut:**
- 2—2½×56" binding strips

## assemble scarf

[1] Referring to **Diagram 1**, sew together long edges of 15 rectangles to make a row. Press seams open. The row should be 6¼×45½" including seam allowances. Repeat to make a second row.

[2] Place one row right side down on a flat surface. Lightly spray wrong side of row with basting spray or dot with glue stick. Place batting on top of row and finger-press. Lightly spray top of batting with basting spray or dot with glue stick. Place second row right side up on batting to complete fabric sandwich (**Diagram 2**). Finger-press.

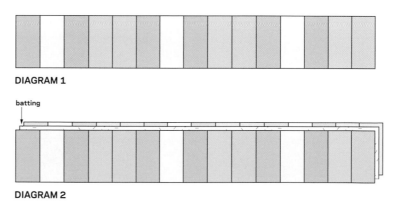

**DIAGRAM 1**

batting

**DIAGRAM 2**

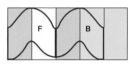

**DIAGRAM 3**

[3] Trace pattern on template plastic and cut out. Mark one side of template as the front and the reverse side as the back.

[4] Referring to **Diagram 3**, place template, front side up, at one end of fabric sandwich. Trace template shape onto row, reversing template after each tracing.

[5] Using shears or a rotary cutter and mat, cut through all layers of fabric sandwich along drawn lines.

[6] Bind with solid light blue binding strips to complete scarf. (For details, see Better Binding, *page 206*.)

To make this toasty version of Warm Fuzzies, we used three assorted colors of Minkee Gelato by Benartex. Make your scarf as long as you want by adding extra 3½×6¼" rectangles to the rows. Be sure to add extra length to binding as well. For a super quick scarf, use a continuous length of fleece for the reverse side.

## tips for working with knit-back fleece

▸ Watch how you cut your pieces. Knit-back fleece tends to stretch crosswise but very little along the lengthwise grain (parallel to the selvages).

▸ Keep a lint roller handy—faux fur fabrics "shed" when cut. If possible, take cut pieces outdoors and shake well before sewing. Or, machine-dry the pieces for a few minutes to remove the "fluffies" or "pills."

▸ Use a walking foot to prevent the fabric from slipping as you sew. Some plush fabric tends to curl when piecing. If needed, use a slightly larger seam allowance (from ⅜" to ½").

▸ Watch the nap of the fabric, especially if you want the cut pieces to smooth out in the same direction.

▸ Use a longer stitch length, such as 3.0 to 3.5 mm, when piecing knit-back or other pile fabric.

▸ Don't be tempted to use an iron. Just finger-press seams open to avoid scorching the fabric.

▸ Machine-baste the edges of your project before applying the binding to provide more stability and make the binding application easier.

▸ Keep your bobbin case clean.

# sweet
# baby kisses

Don't know if it is a boy or a girl? Soft greens, blues, and yellows accent the paisley, dot, stripe, floral, and print fabrics in this cute quilt for a lucky baby boy or girl.

DESIGNER **ELLEN GAFFNEY**
PHOTOGRAPHS **GREG SCHEIDEMANN**

*Babies sometime surprise us by coming earlier than expected. You can be ready with this quick-to-assemble design using assorted baby prints in soft colors and featuring a miniature pocket in the center for tucking in a little stuffed dog.*

- - - - - - - - - - - - - - - - - - - - - - - - - - - - - - - - - - - - - -

## materials

- ½ yard blue dot (blocks, pocket, inner border)
- 1⅔ yards novelty print (blocks, stuffed dog, outer border)
- ¼ yard teal leaf print (blocks, stuffed dog, binding)
- 9×22" piece (fat eighth) each blue-and-green large and small floral (blocks, binding)
- ¼ yard lime-green print (blocks, binding)
- ¼ yard lime-green dot (blocks, binding)
- ¼ yard teal swirl print (blocks, binding)
- ¼ yard multicolor stripe (blocks, binding)
- ¼ yard yellow print (blocks, binding)
- ¼ yard yellow-and-green paisley (blocks, binding)
- ¼ yard yellow-and-green vine print (blocks, binding)
- 3 yards backing fabric
- 50" square batting
- ⅜×6" lime-green grosgrain ribbon
- Polyester fiberfill

Finished quilt: 43½" square
Finished blocks: 12" square

Quantities are for 44/45"-wide, 100% cotton fabrics. Measurements include ¼" seam allowances. Sew with right sides together unless otherwise stated.

## general assembly tips

The blocks for this quilt are pieced using the Courthouse Steps assembly method, in which matching rectangles are added to opposite sides of a center square.

## cut fabrics

To make the best use of your fabrics, cut pieces in the following order. Patterns can be found on *Pattern Sheet 1*. To make pattern templates, see "What Are Templates?" on *page 201*. Cut outer border strips lengthwise (parallel to the selvage).

**From blue dot, cut:**
- 5—1×42" strips for inner border
- 2 of Pattern A

**From novelty print, cut:**
- 4—3½×50½" outer border strips
- 1 of Pattern B

**From teal leaf print, cut:**
- 1 of Pattern B reversed

## cut and assemble block a

**From each blue-and-green floral, cut:**
- 2—6½" squares

**From lime-green print, cut:**
- 2—3½×12½" rectangles
- 2—3½×6½" rectangles

**From lime-green dot, cut:**
- 2—3½×12½" rectangles
- 2—3½×6½" rectangles

**From teal leaf print, cut:**
- 2—3½×12½" rectangles
- 2—3½×6½" rectangles

**From teal swirl print, cut:**
- 2—3½×12½" rectangles
- 2—3½×6½" rectangles

[1] Sew matching 3½×6½" rectangles to opposite edges of a blue-and-green floral 6½" square (**Diagram 1**). Press seams away from center square.

[2] Join matching 3½×12½" rectangles to remaining edges of center square to make Block A. Press seams away from center square.

[3] Repeat steps 1 and 2 to make four total of Block A.

## cut and assemble block b

**From each lime-green print, lime-green dot, teal leaf print, and teal swirl print, cut:**
- 1—3½" square

**From multicolor stripe, cut:**
- 2—3×12½" rectangles
- 2—3×7½" rectangles
- 2—2½×7½" rectangles
- 2—2½×3½" rectangles

**From yellow print, cut:**
- 2—3×12½" rectangles
- 2—3×7½" rectangles
- 2—2½×7½" rectangles
- 2—2½×3½" rectangles

**From yellow-and-green paisley, cut:**
- 2—3×12½" rectangles
- 2—3×7½" rectangles
- 2—2½×7½" rectangles
- 2—2½×3½" rectangles

**From yellow-and-green vine print, cut:**
- 2—3×12½" rectangles
- 2—3×7½" rectangles
- 2—2½×7½" rectangles
- 2—2½×3½" rectangles

[1] Sew matching 2½×3½" rectangles to opposite edges of a 3½" square (**Diagram 2**). Press seams away from center square. Join matching 2½×7½" rectangles to remaining edges of center square. Press seams away from center square.

[2] Referring to **Diagram 2**, join a different set of matching 3×7½" rectangles to opposite edges of center square. Join matching 3×12½" rectangles to remaining edges to make Block B. Press seams away from center square.

[3] Repeat steps 1 and 2 to make four total of Block B.

## cut and assemble block c

**From novelty print, cut:**
▸ 1—8½" square
**From blue dot, cut:**
▸ 2—2½×12½" rectangles
▸ 2—2½×8½" rectangles

[1] Sew blue dot 2½×8½" rectangles to opposite edges of novelty print 8½" square (**Diagram 3**). Press seams away from center square.

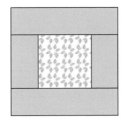

**DIAGRAM 1**

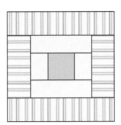

**DIAGRAM 2**

**DIAGRAM 3**

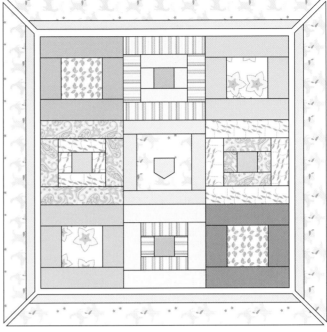

**QUILT ASSEMBLY DIAGRAM**

[2] Join blue dot 2½×12½" rectangles to remaining edges to make one Block C. Press seams away from center square.

## assemble pocket and stuffed dog

[1] Sew pocket A pieces, right sides together, leaving an opening on top edge for turning. Turn right side out. Press.

[2] Place one end of ribbon about ½" into opening; pin or baste in place. Topstitch ¼" from edge all around pocket, securing ribbon.

[3] With right sides together, sew dog-shape B pieces, leaving an opening for turning near dog's belly. Stuff firmly

with fiberfill. Place other end of ribbon about ½" into opening; pin or baste in place. With matching thread, whipstitch opening closed, securing ribbon, to make stuffed dog.

## assemble quilt center

[1] Referring to **Quilt Assembly Diagram** for placement, lay out blocks A, B, and C in three horizontal rows. Sew together blocks in each row. Press seams in one direction, alternating direction with each row.

[2] Join rows to make quilt center. Press seams in one direction. The quilt center should be 36½" square, including seam allowances.

tip
If your stitch quality is poor, lift the presser foot, unthread the machine, and try rethreading it. Often, this is the only fix you need.

## assemble and add borders

[1] Cut and piece blue dot 1×42" strips to make:
  ‣ 4—1×50½" inner border strips

[2] Aligning long edges, join an inner border strip to an outer border strip to make a border unit. Press seam toward outer border strip. Repeat to make four border units total.

[3] Beginning and ending ¼" from quilt center edges, sew border units to opposite edges of quilt center. Repeat to sew border units to remaining edges, mitering corners, to complete quilt top. (For details, see Mitering Borders, *page 208*.) Press all seams toward border units.

## finish quilt

[1] Layer quilt top, batting, and backing; baste. (For details, see Quilt It, *page 197*.)

[2] Quilt as desired. Ellen machine-stitched in the ditch around each block and the inner border. She quilted parallel lines through the center square of Block C.

[3] From remaining assorted print, floral, paisley, dot, and stripe fabrics, cut:
  ‣ 88—2½" squares

[4] Cut and piece assorted 2½" squares to make:
  ‣ 4—2½×44½" pieced binding strips

[5] Bind with pieced binding strips. (For details, see Better Binding, *page 206*.)

## color option

This lively collection of paisleys and prints revs up the contrast on our larger throw version of "Sweet Baby Kisses." Although the same tomato-red paisley is used for the center of each of the 12 blocks, the color placement of the surrounding fabrics is decidedly scrappy. The large size of the blocks makes this the perfect quilt to show off a mix-and-match collection of prints.

QUILTMAKER **DEB SIMDORN**

[6] Referring to **Quilt Assembly Diagram**, *page 151*, place pocket in center of Block C; pin in place. Whipstitch on sides and bottom to secure to quilt top. Tuck stuffed dog into pocket.

160

170

186

165

# more favorites

With a little experience under your belt, you're ready for a little bit more of a challenge. Check out these handpicked favorites that include throws, wall hangings, and bed-size quilts, all with modern flair.

**Dots Are Hot** ............................. 156
**Party Stripes** ........................... 160
**Lunar Eclipse** .......................... 165
**Spring Loaded** ........................ 170
**Cubic Rhythm** ......................... 176
**One-Piece Wonder** ................... 181
**Color Fun Daisies** ...................... 186

# dots are hot

DESIGNER **VALORI WELLS**
PHOTOGRAPHS **CAMERON SADEGHPOUR**

## Simple shapes make a strong statement on this throw full of all things circular.

*The appliqué circles on this fun and colorful quilt are secured using a simple blind-hem stitch. A palette of 18 solid fabrics provides plenty of options for playing with color combinations in each block.*

*Yardages and instructions given are for cutting all circle appliqués in the same step. (To conserve fabric, first cut and appliqué only the largest circles. Then use the circles trimmed from the appliqué foundations to cut the next-smaller-size circles. To use this method, you'll need 8¼ yards total of assorted solids.)*

## materials

- 1¼ yards solid red (blocks, binding)
- 9⅜ yards total assorted solids (blocks)
- 4⅞ yards backing fabric
- 71×87" batting
- Freezer paper
- Glue stick
- Clear monofilament thread

Finished quilt: 64½×80½"
Finished block: 8" square

Quantities are for 44/45"-wide, 100% cotton fabrics. Measurements include a ¼" seam allowance. Sew with right sides together unless otherwise stated.

**tip** To punch up the circles, consider machine-appliquéing them in place with contrasting thread. Heavyweight black thread would provide folk-art-style contrast.

## cut fabrics

To make the best use of your fabrics, cut pieces in the following order. Circle patterns can be found on *Pattern Sheet 1*.

This quilt was made using a freezer-paper method on the fabric's wrong side for appliquéing. The instructions that follow are for this technique. For tips on perfecting your appliqué skills, see "Better Blind-Hem Appliqué," *page 159*.

To use freezer paper for preparing appliqué shapes, complete these steps.

[1] Lay freezer paper, shiny side down, over circle patterns A–D. Use a pencil to trace each pattern the number of times indicated in cutting instructions, leaving ½" between tracings. Cut out each freezer-paper circle on the traced line to make freezer-paper templates. (To save time, Valori cuts fewer freezer-paper templates than specified, reusing each one five or six times.)

## APPLIQUÉ PLACEMENT DIAGRAMS

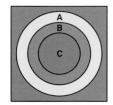

**BLOCK 1**

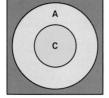

**BLOCK 2**

**BLOCK 3**

**BLOCK 4**

**BLOCK 5**

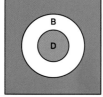

**BLOCK 6**

**BLOCK 7**

**BLOCK PLACEMENT DIAGRAM**

---

[2] Using a hot, dry iron, press freezer-paper templates, shiny side down, onto wrong sides of designated fabrics; let cool. Cut out each fabric circle, adding a ¼" seam allowance. Do not remove the freezer paper.

[3] On each fabric circle, run a glue stick along the wrong side of the seam allowance. Use your fingertips to fold the seam allowances under and press against the freezer paper; let dry.

**From solid red, cut:**

▸ 8—2½×42" binding strips

**From remaining solid red and the assorted solids, cut:**

▸ 80—8½" squares
▸ 43 of Pattern A
▸ 51 of Pattern C
▸ 69 of Pattern B
▸ 42 of Pattern D

## appliqué blocks

[1] Center and pin a prepared solid A circle appliqué on a contrasting solid 8½" square appliqué foundation. Using clear monofilament thread, blind-hem-stitch around the A circle (see "Better Blind-Hem Appliqué," opposite, for details and tips).

[2] Carefully trim excess foundation fabric from behind the appliqué, leaving a ½" seam allowance. Dampen the exposed freezer-paper template with a spray bottle. After five minutes, peel away freezer paper and discard. (To easily release freezer paper from fabric, gently pull block on diagonal.) Press appliqué foundation from both sides until fabric is dry.

[3] Repeat steps 1 and 2 to add a prepared solid B circle appliqué then a C circle appliqué to the appliqué foundation to complete a Block 1 (**Appliqué Placement Diagrams**).

[4] Repeat steps 1 through 3 to make 21 total of Block 1.

[5] Referring to the **Appliqué Placement Diagrams** for the appropriate circles to use and always working from the biggest circle to the smallest, repeat steps 1 and 2 to make:
- 11 of Block 2
- 8 of Block 3
- 3 of Block 4
- 5 of Block 5
- 18 of Block 6
- 14 of Block 7

## assemble quilt top

[1] Referring to the **Block Placement Diagram**, lay out the blocks in 10 horizontal rows.

[2] Sew together blocks in each row. Press seams in one direction, alternating direction with each row. Join rows to complete quilt top. Press seams in one direction.

## finish quilt

[1] Layer quilt top, batting, and backing; baste. (For details, see Quilt It, *page 197*.)

[2] Quilt as desired. This quilt was machine-quilted with a large spiral on each stack of circle appliqués and a smaller spiral over each point where four blocks come together.

[3] Bind with solid red binding strips. (For details, see Better Binding, *page 206*.)

## color option

A single-size, repetitive circle stitched in a positive-negative pattern repeat lends a calming influence to this table runner that is in stark contrast to the "Dots are Hot" quilt.

This two-block-wide version can be modified to fit any length table. To make it super quick and easy, use fusible web and machine-appliqué the Pattern B circles in place. Skip the batting and quilting phases, and your runner will drape beautifully over the table edge. Sewing with right sides together, add a same-size backing, leaving an opening for turning. Turn right side out, then slip-stitch the opening closed.

## better blind-hem appliqué

- Designer Valori Wells recommends using a size 60/8 embroidery needle in the machine, clear monofilament thread for the needle, and 60-weight embroidery thread for the bobbin.

- Set up your machine for a narrow, short blind-hem stitch, setting the width and length at 1 mm if possible. A blind-hem stitch takes several straight stitches forward, one zigzag stitch, several more straight stitches, and another zigzag stitch (see diagram at right).

- When sewing, the straight stitches of the blind-hem stitch should go into the foundation fabric right alongside the appliqué, and the zigzag stitches should catch the appliqué edges.

**BLIND-HEM STITCH**

# party stripes

If you can sew a straight line, you'll have great luck with this strip-pieced quilt full of color. **DESIGNER KRIS KERRIGAN** **PHOTOGRAPHS CAMERON SADEGHPOUR**

*Construction for this vivid quilt couldn't be easier. First piece chunks of fabric together. Then cut pieced-together strips for a random, free-spirited look. Sew the strips, add a border, and hand- or machine-quilt to finish in no time. Once you try it, fast and precise stripping is sure to become your new favorite method to make a quilt.*

## materials

- 3—18×22" pieces (fat quarters) assorted lime green prints (strips)
- 2—18×22" pieces (fat quarters) assorted orange prints (strips)
- 18×22" piece (fat quarter) each cream and red prints (strips)
- 2—18×22" pieces (fat quarters) assorted yellow prints (strips)
- ½ yard each assorted yellow, purple, royal blue, and light pink prints (strips)
- 3—18×22" pieces (fat quarters) assorted bright pink prints (strips)

- 4—18×22" pieces (fat quarters) assorted turquoise prints (strips)
- 5¼ yards blue stripe (border, binding, backing)
- 60×83" batting

Finished quilt: 54½×75½"

Quantities are for 44/45"-wide, 100% cotton fabrics. Measurements include a ¼" seam allowance. Sew with right sides together unless otherwise stated.

## cut fabrics

To make the best use of your fabrics, cut the pieces in the order that follows. Cut border strips lengthwise (parallel to the selvage).

**From assorted lime green prints, cut:**
- 1—10½×15" rectangle for strip 30
- 1—9½×15" rectangle for strip 14
- 1—8½×15" rectangle for strip 18
- 1—6½×9" rectangle for strip 1

**From assorted orange prints, cut:**
- 1—16½×15" rectangle for strip 22
- 1—10½×15" rectangle for strip 13
- 1—9½×9" rectangle for strip 2

**From cream print, cut:**
- 1—8½×9" rectangle for strip 3

**From red print, cut:**
- 1—12½×15" rectangle for strip 24
- 1—8½×15" rectangle for strip 10

**From assorted yellow prints, cut:**
- 1—16½×15" rectangle for strip 11
- 1—12½×15" rectangle for strip 27
- 1—10½×15" rectangle for strip 29
- 1—8½×15" rectangle for strip 8
- 1—11½×9" rectangle for strip 5

**tip** For smooth, even, and undistorted long seams, alternate the sewing direction of the rows when assembling the quilt center. Sew one row left to right, the next right to left.

**DIAGRAM 1**

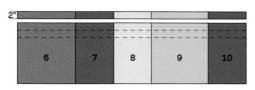

**DIAGRAM 2**

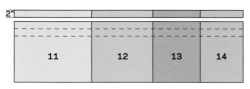

**DIAGRAM 3**

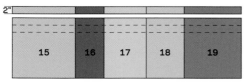

**DIAGRAM 4**

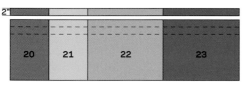

**DIAGRAM 5**

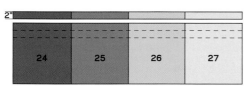

**DIAGRAM 6**

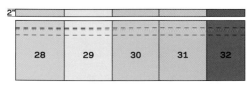

**DIAGRAM 7**

**From purple print, cut:**
- 1—14½×9" rectangle for strip 4
- 1—8½×15" rectangle for strip 20

**From royal blue print, cut:**
- 3—12½×15" rectangles for strips 6, 19, and 25

**From light pink print, cut:**
- 1—13½×15" rectangle for strip 15
- 1—10½×15" rectangle for strip 31

**From assorted bright pink prints, cut:**
- 1—16½×15" rectangle for strip 23
- 2—8½×15" rectangles for strips 7 and 32
- 1—6½×15" rectangle for strip 16

**From assorted turquoise prints, cut:**
- 1—13½×15" rectangle for strip 12
- 2—12½×15" rectangles for strips 9 and 26
- 1—10½×15" rectangle for strip 28
- 1—9½×15" rectangle for strip 17
- 1—8½×15" rectangle for strip 21

**From blue stripe, cut:**
- 7—2½×42" binding strips
- 2—3½×85" border strips
- 2—3½×64" border strips

## assemble units and segments

[1] Referring to **Diagram 1**, join rectangles 1 through 5 into a 48½×9" unit. Press seams in one direction. Cut unit into four 48½×2" Unit 1 segments.

[2] Referring to **Diagram 2**, join rectangles 6 through 10 into a 48½×15" unit. Press seams in one direction. Cut unit into seven 48½×2" Unit 2 segments.

[3] Sew together rectangles 11 through 14 into a 48½×15" unit (**Diagram 3**). Press seams in one direction. Cut unit into seven 48½×2" Unit 3 segments.

[4] Referring to **Diagram 4**, join rectangles 15 through 19 into a 48½×15" unit. Press seams in one direction. Cut unit into seven 48½×2" Unit 4 segments.

[5] Sew together rectangles 20 through 23 into a 48½×15" unit (**Diagram 5**). Press seams in one direction. Cut unit into seven 48½×2" Unit 5 segments.

[6] Referring to **Diagram 6**, join rectangles 24 through 27 into a 48½×15" unit. Press seams in one direction. Cut unit into seven 48½×2" Unit 6 segments.

[7] Sew together rectangles 28 through 32 into a 48½×15" unit (**Diagram 7**). Press seams in one direction. Cut unit into seven 48½×2" Unit 7 segments.

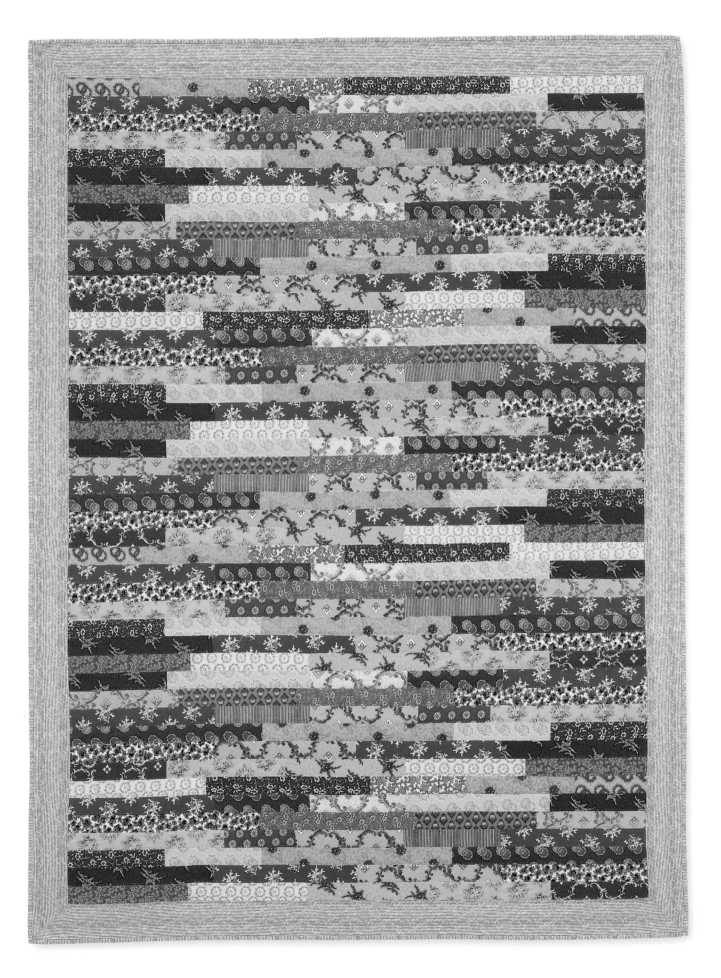

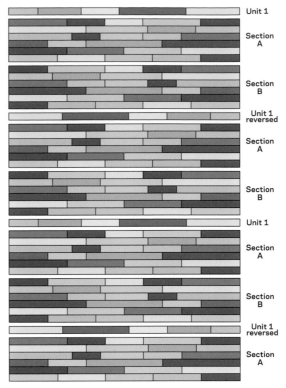

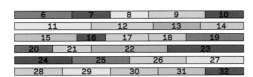

**DIAGRAM 8 – SECTION A**

**DIAGRAM 9 – SECTION B**

**QUILT ASSEMBLY DIAGRAM**

## assemble quilt top

[1] Referring to **Diagram 8**, join one segment from each of units 2 through 7 to make Section A. Press seams in one direction. Section A should be 48½×9½" including seam allowances. Repeat to make four total of Section A.

[2] Referring to **Diagram 9**, sew together one segment from each of units 2 through 7 (in reverse order from Section A) to make Section B. Press seams in one direction. Section B should be 48½×9½" including seam allowances. Repeat to make three total of Section B.

[3] Referring to **Quilt Assembly Diagram** for placement, join four of Section A, three of Section B, and four Unit 1 segments to make quilt center; alternate sections A and B and reverse two of Unit 1 as shown. Press seams in one direction. The quilt center should be 48½×69½" including seam allowances.

## add border

Beginning and ending ¼" from quilt center edges, sew short border strips to short edges of quilt center. Repeat to add long border strips to remaining edges, mitering the corners, to complete quilt top. (For details, see Mitering Borders, *page 208*.) Press all seams toward border.

## finish quilt

[1] Layer quilt top, batting, and backing according to instructions in Quilt It on *page 197*.

[2] Quilt as desired. This quilt was hand-quilted ¼" from each horizontal seam. On the border, two parallel lines were stitched about 1½" apart to give the border texture and depth.

[3] Bind with blue stripe binding strips. (For details, see Better Binding, *page 206*.)

Layer simple-to-sew
Four-Patch blocks
with machine-
appliquéd circles.

# lunar
## eclipse

DESIGNER **JANET HOUTS**
PHOTOGRAPHS **CAMERON SADEGHPOUR**

*Easy to piece; easy to quilt. Punctuate your wall with a sphere of appliquéd moons on a background of small and large Four-Patch blocks.*

## materials

- ¾ yard teal print (Four-Patch blocks)
- ¾ yard teal floral (Four-Patch blocks)
- ¾ yard black print (appliqué blocks)
- ¾ yard teal-and-white print (appliqué blocks)
- ⅔ yard green floral (appliqués)
- ½ yard green stripe (inner border)
- 1⅜ yards black-and-teal check (outer border)
- ⅝ yard teal stripe (binding)
- 4 yards backing fabric
- 70" square batting
- Lightweight fusible web

Finished quilt: 63½" square
Finished blocks: 6" square; 12" square

Quantities are for 44/45"-wide, 100% cotton fabrics. Measurements include ¼" seam allowances. Sew with right sides together unless otherwise stated.

tip

Place 12 equidistant marks around the edge of each circle appliqué, as if placing numbers on a clock face. As you stitch, stop the machine at each mark and pivot the fabric.

## cut fabrics

Cut pieces in the following order. Circle Pattern is found on *Pattern Sheet 1*. To use fusible web for appliquéing, complete the following steps. (For more information on fusible appliqué, see Piece and Appliqué, *page 195*.)

[1] Lay fusible web, paper side up, over patterns. Use a pencil to trace the Circle Pattern nine times, leaving ½" between tracings. Cut out each fusible-web circle roughly ¼" outside traced lines. To avoid stiffness in centers of appliqués, cut out inner portion of each fusible-web circle to about ⅜" from outer edge to make a ring.

[2] Following manufacturer's instructions, press fusible-web rings onto wrong side of green floral; let cool. Cut out circles on drawn lines; peel off paper backings.

**From teal print, cut:**
- 6—3½×42" strips

**From teal floral, cut:**
- 6—3½×42" strips

**From black print, cut:**
- 3—6½×42" strips

**From teal-and-white print, cut:**
- 3—6½×42" strips

**From green floral, cut:**
- 9 of Circle Pattern

**From green stripe, cut:**
- 5—2×42" strips for inner border

**From black-and-teal check, cut:**
- 6—6½×42" strips for outer border

**From teal stripe, cut:**
- 7—2½×42" binding strips

## assemble four-patch blocks

[1] Sew together a teal print 3½×42" strip and a teal floral 3½×42" strip to make a strip set (**Diagram 1**). Press seam toward teal print. Repeat to make six strip sets total. Cut strip sets into 56—3½"-wide segments.

[2] Sew together two 3½"-wide segments to make a Four-Patch block (**Diagram 2**). Press seam in one direction. The Four-Patch block should be 6½" square including seam allowances. Repeat to make 28 Four-Patch blocks total.

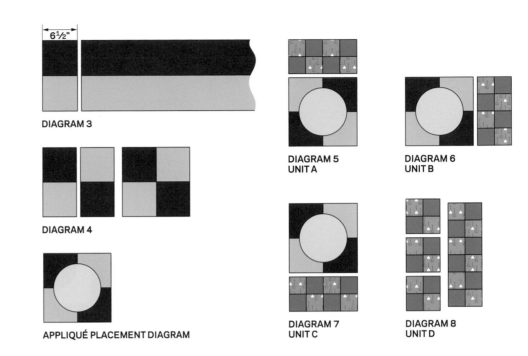

DIAGRAM 3

DIAGRAM 4

APPLIQUÉ PLACEMENT DIAGRAM

DIAGRAM 1

DIAGRAM 2

DIAGRAM 5
UNIT A

DIAGRAM 6
UNIT B

DIAGRAM 7
UNIT C

DIAGRAM 8
UNIT D

## assemble appliqué blocks

[1] Sew together a black print 6½×42" strip and a teal-and-white print 6½×42" strip to make a strip set (Diagram 3). Press seam toward black print. Repeat to make three strip sets total. Cut strip sets into 18—6½"-wide segments.

[2] Sew together two 6½"-wide segments to make an appliqué foundation (Diagram 4). Press seam in one direction. The appliqué foundation should be 12½" square including seam allowances. Repeat to make nine appliqué foundations total.

[3] Center a green floral circle on an appliqué foundation; fuse in place (Appliqué Placement Diagram). Using a narrow zigzag or blind hem stitch, machine-appliqué around edge of circle to make an appliqué block.

The appliqué block should still be 12½" square including seam allowances. (For more information on stitching curved appliqué edges, see "Better Machine Appliqué," page 205, and Tip on page 166.) Repeat to make nine appliqué blocks total.

## assemble units

Refer to specified diagram to make each unit, paying close attention to the positions of the Four-Patch and appliqué blocks.

[1] Join two Four-Patch blocks in a horizontal row (Diagram 5). Press seam in one direction. Join Four-Patch row to top edge of appliqué block to make unit A. Press seam toward appliqué block. Repeat to make four total of unit A.

[2] Join two Four-Patch blocks in a vertical row (Diagram 6). Press seam in one direction. Join Four-Patch row to right-hand edge of appliqué block to make unit B. Press seam toward appliqué block. Repeat to make a second unit B.

[3] Join two Four-Patch blocks in a horizontal row (Diagram 7). Press seam in one direction. Join Four-Patch row to bottom edge of appliqué block to make unit C. Press seam toward appliqué block. Repeat to make a second unit C.

[4] Join three Four-Patch blocks in a vertical row to make unit D (Diagram 8). Press seams in one direction. Repeat to make four total of unit D.

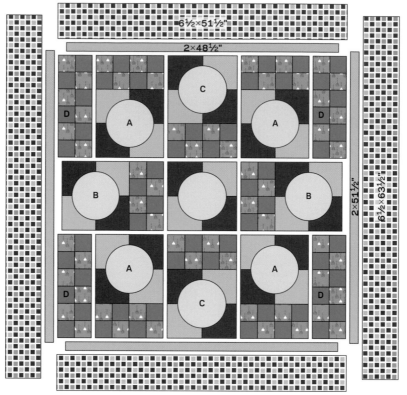

**QUILT ASSEMBLY DIAGRAM**

## assemble quilt center

[1] Referring to **Quilt Assembly Diagram**, lay out units A, B, C, and D and the remaining appliqué block in three horizontal rows. Sew together pieces in each row. Press seams in one direction, alternating direction with each row.

[2] Join rows to make quilt center. Press seams in one direction. The quilt center should be 48½" square including seam allowances.

## add borders

[1] Cut and piece green stripe 2×42" strips to make:
  ‣ 2—2×51½" inner border strips
  ‣ 2—2×48½" inner border strips

[2] Join short inner border strips to opposite edges of quilt center. Add long inner border strips to remaining edges. Press all seams toward inner border.

[3] Cut and piece black-and-teal check 6½×42" strips to make:
  ‣ 2—6½×63½" outer border strips
  ‣ 2—6½×51½" outer border strips

[4] Join short outer border strips to opposite edges of quilt center. Add long outer border strips to remaining edges to complete quilt top. Press all seams toward outer border.

## finish quilt

[1] Layer quilt top, batting, and backing; baste. (For details, see Quilt It, *page 197*.)

[2] Quilt as desired. Machine-quilter Margie Kraft stitched a swirl inside each circle and leaf motifs outside the appliqués. She quilted wavy diagonal lines in the Four-Patch blocks, a loop design in the inner border, and parallel lines in the outer border.

[3] Bind with teal stripe binding strips. (For details, see Better Binding, *page 206*.)

# spring
## loaded

Brighten up your day with the potted flowers in this simple throw showcasing just a hint of appliqué. DESIGNER **BARBARA JONES OF QUILTSOUP**
PHOTOGRAPHS **GREG SCHEIDEMANN**

*The potted flowers on this quilt are stitched using a bevy of cheerful fabrics, which are certain to brighten the decor of any room. The blocks are easy to make in three units: the flower, the stem with leaves, and the pot.*

## materials

- 9×22" piece (fat eighth) white polka dot (blocks)
- ⅜ yard solid white (blocks)
- 18×22" piece (fat quarter) pink polka dot (blocks)
- ½ yard red print (blocks)
- 18×22" piece (fat quarter) yellow polka dot (blocks)
- ¼ yard orange polka dot (blocks)
- 18×22" piece (fat quarter) yellow print (blocks)
- ⅓ yard purple stripe (appliqués, blocks)
- ⅝ yard lime green stripe (blocks, border)
- ½ yard lime green polka dot (appliqués, border)
- 9×22" piece (fat eighth) large turquoise polka dot (appliqués)

- ⅜ yard large green polka dot (appliqués, border)
- 9×22" piece (fat eighth) lime green print (appliqués)
- 2 yards large white polka dot (blocks, border, binding)
- 3¾ yards backing fabric
- 67" square batting
- Freezer paper
- Glue stick

Finished quilt: 61½" square

Quantities are for 44/45"-wide, 100% cotton fabrics.
Measurements include a ¼" seam allowance. Sew with right sides together unless otherwise stated.

## cut fabrics

To make the best use of your fabrics, cut pieces in the following order. Patterns can be found on *Pattern Sheet 1*. To make and use templates for cutting pieces C and D, see "What are Templates?" on *page 201*.

To use freezer paper for preparing appliqué shapes A and B, complete the following steps.

[1] Lay freezer paper, shiny side down, over patterns A and B. Use a pencil to trace each pattern the number of times indicated in cutting instructions, leaving ¼" between tracings. Cut out each freezer-paper shape on the traced line to make freezer-paper templates.

**tip** Secure seams that will not be sewn across again (such as those in border units) and seams that are not sewn to the edge of the fabric (as with inset seams) with a few backstitches on top of previous stitching at both the beginning and the end.

[**2**] Using a hot, dry iron, press freezer-paper templates, shiny side down, onto wrong sides of designated fabrics; let cool. Cut out each fabric piece, adding a ¼" seam allowance. Do not remove the freezer paper.

[**3**] On each fabric piece, run a glue stick along the wrong side of the seam allowance. Using your fingertips, fold over the seam allowance and finger-press it to back of freezer paper. Let dry.

**From white polka dot, cut:**
▸ 16—2" squares
**From solid white, cut:**
▸ 8—4⅜×6½" rectangles
▸ 4 each of patterns D and D reversed
▸ 36—2" squares
**From pink polka dot, cut:**
▸ 8—5" squares
**From red print, cut:**
▸ 1—5×42" strip
▸ 12—5" squares
**From yellow polka dot, cut:**
▸ 8—5" squares
**From orange polka dot, cut:**
▸ 1—2×42" strip
▸ 8—5" squares
**From yellow print, cut:**
▸ 8—5" squares
**From purple stripe, cut:**
▸ 8—5" squares
▸ 3 of Pattern A

**From lime green stripe, cut:**
▸ 12—5½×9½" rectangles
▸ 4—1¾×6½" rectangles
**From lime green polka dot, cut:**
▸ 8—5½×9½" rectangles
▸ 4 of Pattern B
▸ 2 of Pattern A
**From large turquoise polka dot, cut:**
▸ 4 of Pattern A
**From large green polka dot, cut:**
▸ 4—5½×8½" rectangles
▸ 4—3½×5½" rectangles
▸ 4 of Pattern A
**From lime green print, cut:**
▸ 4 of Pattern B
**From large white polka dot, cut:**
▸ 7—2½×42" binding strips
▸ 8—9½×12½" rectangles
▸ 4—3½×12½" rectangles
▸ 4—3½×9½" rectangles
▸ 40—2½" squares

## assemble units

[1] Mark a diagonal line on wrong sides of white polka dot 2" squares and solid white 2" squares. (To prevent fabric from stretching, place 220-grit sandpaper under squares.)

[2] Align a marked white polka dot 2" square in one corner of a pink polka dot 5" square (**Diagram 1**; note direction of drawn line). Stitch on line; trim excess fabric,

leaving ¼" seam allowance. (Barbara recommends stitching just inside the line.) Press open attached triangle to make a flower quarter. Repeat to make four flower quarters total.

[3] Referring to **Diagram 2**, sew together flower quarters in pairs. Press seams in opposite directions. Join pairs to make a flower unit. Press seam in one direction. The flower unit should be 9½" square including seam allowances.

[4] Repeat steps 2 and 3 with red print 5" squares and remaining white polka dot 2" squares to make three flower units.

[5] Repeat steps 2 and 3 with yellow polka dot, orange polka dot, yellow print, and purple stripe 5" squares and the solid white 2" squares to make nine flower units.

[6] Sew solid white 4⅜×6½" rectangles to long edges of a lime green stripe 1¾×6½" rectangle to make a stem unit (**Diagram 3**). Press seams toward lime green stripe. The stem unit should be 6½×9½" including seam allowances. Repeat to make four stem units total.

[7] Sew together an orange polka dot 2×42" strip and a red print 5×42" strip to make a strip set (Diagram 4). Press seam toward red strip. Referring to Diagram 4, cut four of Pattern C from strip set.

[8] Sew solid white D and D reversed triangles to opposite edges of C flowerpot to make a flowerpot unit. Press seams toward C piece. The flowerpot unit should be 6½×9½" including seam allowances. Repeat to make four flowerpot units total.

## appliqué units

[1] Center and baste a lime green polka dot A flower center on a pink flower unit (Diagram 5). Using lime green thread, machine-appliqué around A circle.

[2] Carefully trim excess fabric from behind appliqué, leaving a ¼" seam allowance. Dampen exposed freezer-paper template with a spray bottle. After five minutes, peel away freezer paper and discard. (To easily release freezer paper from fabric, gently pull unit diagonally.) Press appliquéd flower unit from both sides until fabric is dry.

[3] Referring to Quilt Assembly Diagram for color placement, repeat steps 1 and 2 to appliqué an A flower center to each remaining flower unit.

[4] Referring to Diagram 6, lay out a lime green polka dot B leaf and a lime green print B leaf on a stem unit; baste in place. Using lime green thread, machine-appliqué around each leaf. Trim excess fabric from behind appliqué and remove freezer paper as done in Step 2 to make an appliquéd stem unit. Repeat to make four appliquéd stem units total.

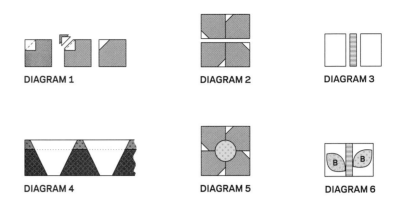

DIAGRAM 1    DIAGRAM 2    DIAGRAM 3

DIAGRAM 4    DIAGRAM 5    DIAGRAM 6

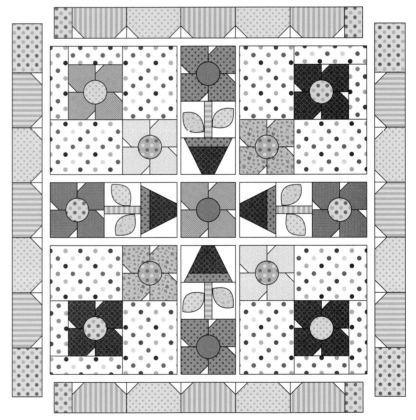

QUILT ASSEMBLY DIAGRAM

**tip** Use a lined index card to measure your seam allowances when you don't have a ruler or graph paper available. The lines are exactly ¼" apart.

## assemble blocks

[1] Sew a large white polka dot 3½×9½" rectangle to top edge of a pink flower unit (**Diagram 7**). Press seam toward white rectangle.

[2] Add a large white polka dot 3½×12½" rectangle to left-hand edge of the flower unit to make a pink quarter flower block (**Diagram 8**). Press seam toward white rectangle.

[3] Repeat steps 1 and 2 with three red flower units to make three red quarter flower blocks.

[4] Lay out a pink quarter flower block, a yellow polka dot flower unit, and two large white polka dot 9½×12½" rectangles in pairs (**Diagram 9**). Sew together each pair. Press seams in opposite directions. Join pairs to make a flower block. Press seam in one direction. The flower block should be 21½" square including seam allowances.

[5] Referring to **Quilt Assembly Diagram**, *page 173*, for color placement, repeat Step 4 to make four flower blocks total.

[6] Lay out an orange flower unit, a stem unit, and a flowerpot unit in a vertical row (**Diagram 10**). Sew together pieces to make a flowerpot block. Press seams in one direction. The flowerpot block should be 9½×21½" including seam allowances. Repeat with a second orange flower unit and two purple flower units to make four flowerpot blocks total.

## assemble quilt center

[1] Referring to **Quilt Assembly Diagram**, lay out four flower blocks, four flowerpot blocks, and remaining pink flower unit in three horizontal rows.

[2] Sew together pieces in each row. Press seams toward flower blocks or flower unit. Join rows to make quilt center. Press seams in one direction. The quilt center should be 51½" square including seam allowances.

## assemble and add border

[1] Mark a diagonal line on wrong sides of large white polka dot 2½" squares.

[2] Align a marked large white polka dot 2½" square in left corner of a lime green stripe 5½×9½" rectangle (**Diagram 11**; note direction of drawn line). Stitch on line; trim excess fabric, leaving ¼" seam allowance. Press open attached triangle.

[3] In same manner, align a second marked large white polka dot 2½" square in adjacent corner of rectangle. Stitch on line; trim and press as before to make a lime green stripe border rectangle.

[4] Repeat steps 2 and 3 to make 12 lime green stripe border rectangles and eight lime green polka dot border rectangles total.

[5] Referring to **Quilt Assembly Diagram**, lay out three lime green stripe border rectangles, two lime green polka dot border rectangles, and two large green

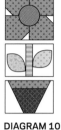
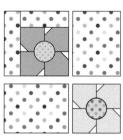

**DIAGRAM 7**  **DIAGRAM 8**  **DIAGRAM 9**  **DIAGRAM 10**  **DIAGRAM 11**

polka dot 3½×5½" rectangles in a row. Sew together pieces to make a short border unit. Press seams in one direction. The short border unit should be 5½×51½" including seam allowances. Repeat to make a second short border unit.

[6] Referring to **Quilt Assembly Diagram**, lay out three lime green stripe border rectangles, two lime green polka dot border rectangles, and two large green polka dot 5½×8½" rectangles in a row. Sew pieces together to make a long border unit. Press seams in one direction. The long border unit should be 5½×61½" including seam allowances. Repeat to make a second long border unit.

[7] Sew short border units to top and bottom edges of quilt center. Sew long border units to side edges to complete quilt top. Press all seams toward border units.

## finish quilt

[1] Layer quilt top, batting, and backing; baste. (For details, see Quilt It, *page 197*.)

[2] Quilt as desired. This quilt was stitched with a loopy design in the block backgrounds and an abstract flower design in each border rectangle. A spiral was stitched in each flower center, a swirl leaf design in each flower petal and leaf, a flower with a leaf in each flowerpot, and a wavy line in each stem.

[3] Bind with large white polka dot binding strips. (For details, see Better Binding, *page 206*.)

# cubic rhythm

DESIGNER **DEBBIE MADDY OF CALICO CARRIAGE QUILT DESIGNS**
PHOTOGRAPHS **ADAM ALBRIGHT**

Alternating bold prints and tone-on-tones creates a simple, graphic quilt.

*The small and large prints alternating with a green tone-on-tone give this easy-to-assemble quilt its texture and tempo. Two floral borders frame just five 15"-square blocks and two 15×30" blocks to create this offbeat throw that's a perfect project for beginners but interesting enough to intrigue quilters of all levels.*

## materials

- ¾ yard brown print (blocks)
- ¾ yard pink tone-on-tone (blocks)
- ¾ yard multicolor print (blocks)
- 1¼ yards green polka dot (blocks, binding)
- ⅝ yard light green tone-on-tone (blocks)
- ⅞ yard green tone-on-tone (inner border)
- 2 yards brown-and-pink floral (outer border)
- 4⅛ yards backing fabric
- 72" square batting

Finished quilt: 65½" square
Finished blocks: block A, 15×30"; block B, 15" square

Quantities are for 44/45"-wide, 100% cotton fabrics. Measurements include ¼" seam allowances. Sew with right sides together unless otherwise stated.

## cut fabrics

Cut pieces in the following order. Cut outer border strips lengthwise (parallel to the selvages).

**From brown print, cut:**
- 3—4½×15½" rectangles
- 3—4½×11½" rectangles
- 2—3½×18½" rectangles
- 3—2½×11½" rectangles
- 3—2½×9½" rectangles

**From pink tone-on-tone, cut:**
- 2—4½×9½" rectangles
- 2—4½×5½" rectangles
- 2—3½×18½" rectangles
- 2—3½×8½" rectangles
- 2—2½×18½" rectangles
- 2—2½×8½" rectangles
- 2—2½×5½" rectangles
- 2—2½×3½" rectangles

**From multicolor print, cut:**
- 2—5½×23½" rectangles
- 2—5½×15½" rectangles
- 2—2½×23½" rectangles
- 2—2½×15½" rectangles

**tip** Make this quick-to-piece quilt in a larger size by simply stitching a few more blocks. Try adding another row of B blocks to the quilt for a good-size throw.

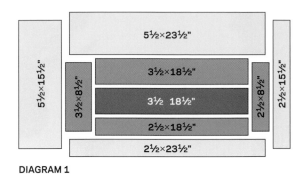

**DIAGRAM 1**

Labels in Diagram 1:
- 5½×23½"
- 3½×18½"
- 3½ 18½"
- 2½×18½"
- 2½×23½"
- 5½×15½"
- 3½×8½"
- 2½×8½"
- 2½×15½"

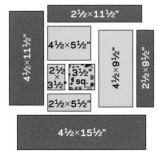

**DIAGRAM 2**

Labels in Diagram 2:
- 2½×11½"
- 4½×11½"
- 4½×5½"
- 2½×3½"
- 3½" sq.
- 4½×9½"
- 2½×9½"
- 2½×5½"
- 4½×15½"

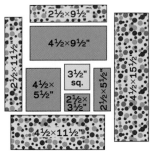

**DIAGRAM 3**

Labels in Diagram 3:
- 2½×9½"
- 4½×9½"
- 2½×11½"
- 4½×5½"
- 3½" sq.
- 2½×3½"
- 2½×5½"
- 4½×15½"
- 4½×11½"

---

**From green polka dot, cut:**
- ▸ 7—2½×42" binding strips
- ▸ 2—4½×15½" rectangles
- ▸ 2—4½×11½" rectangles
- ▸ 3—3½" squares
- ▸ 2—2½×11½" rectangles
- ▸ 2—2½×9½" rectangles

**From light green tone-on-tone, cut:**
- ▸ 3—4½×9½" rectangles
- ▸ 3—4½×5½" rectangles
- ▸ 2—3½" squares
- ▸ 3—2½×5½" rectangles
- ▸ 3—2½×3½" rectangles

**From green tone-on-tone, cut:**
- ▸ 6—3½×42" strips for inner border

**From brown-and-pink floral, cut:**
- ▸ 2—7½×65½" outer border strips
- ▸ 2—7½×51½" outer border strips

## assemble block a

[1] Referring to **Diagram 1**, lay out brown print, pink tone-on-tone, and multicolor print rectangles in the sizes shown. Sew together brown print and pink tone-on-tone rectangles in sections to make center unit. Press seams toward pink tone-on-tone rectangles.

[2] Join multicolor print rectangles to center unit to make block A. Press seams toward multicolor print rectangles. Block A should be 15½×30½" including seam allowances.

[3] Repeat steps 1 and 2 to make a second block A.

## assemble block b

[1] Referring to **Diagram 2**, lay out a green polka dot square, light green tone-on-tone rectangles, and brown print rectangles in

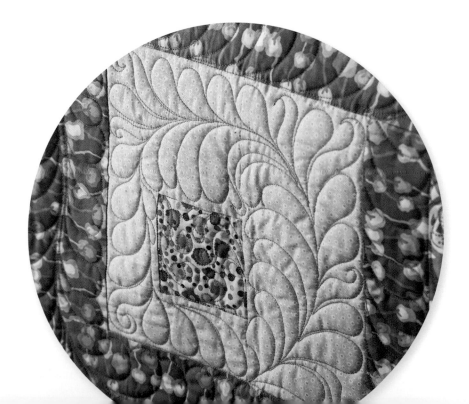

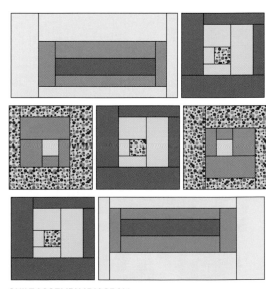

**QUILT ASSEMBLY DIAGRAM**

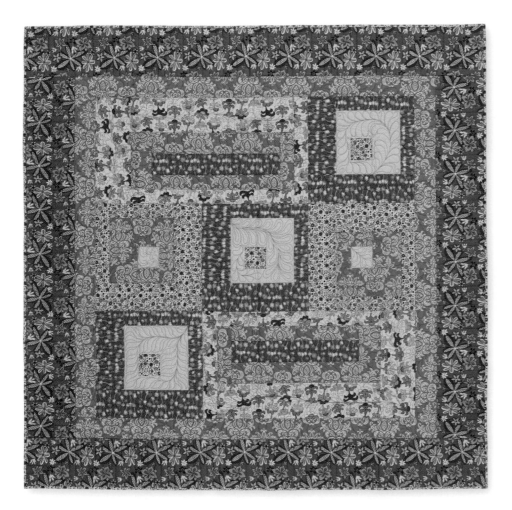

the sizes shown. Sew together green polka dot square and light green tone-on-tone rectangles in sections to make center unit. Press seams toward light green tone-on-tone rectangles.

[2] Join brown print rectangles to center unit to make a brown block B. Press seams toward brown print rectangles. Block B should be 15½" square including seam allowances.

[3] Repeat steps 1 and 2 to make three brown B blocks total.

[4] Referring to **Diagram 3**, repeat steps 1 and 2 using light green tone-on-tone squares, pink tone-on-tone rectangles, and green

polka dot rectangles in the sizes shown to make two green B blocks total.

## assemble quilt center

[1] Lay out A blocks and B blocks in three horizontal rows (**Quilt Assembly Diagram**; note rotation of the blocks).

[2] Sew together blocks in each row. Press seams in one direction, alternating direction with each row.

[3] Join rows to complete quilt center. Press seams in one direction. The quilt center should be 45½" square including seam allowances.

## add borders

[1] Cut and piece green tone-on-tone 3½×42" strips to make:
  ‣ 2—3½×51½" inner border strips
  ‣ 2—3½×45½" inner border strips

[2] Sew short inner border strips to opposite edges of quilt center. Join long inner border strips to remaining edges. Press all seams toward inner border.

[3] Sew short outer border strips to opposite edges of quilt center. Add long outer border strips to remaining edges to complete quilt top. Press all seams toward outer border.

## finish quilt

[1] Layer quilt top, batting, and backing; baste. (For details, see Quilt It, *page 197*.)

[2] Quilt as desired. This quilt was stitched with feather motifs in the blocks and inner border, and parallel lines in the outer border.

[3] Bind with green polka dot binding strips. (For details, see Better Binding, *page 206*.)

# color option

When you're feeling timid about selecting colors and prints for a quilt, choose fabrics from a single fabric collection to guarantee success. Coordinating solids, florals, and small prints from a citrus-inspired collection were used for this version of Cubic Rhythm.

PHOTOGRAPH **GREG SCHEIDEMANN**

Who'd ever guess this playful throw is easily sewn row by row?

QUILTMAKER **MARY PEPPER**
PHOTOGRAPHS **GREG SCHEIDEMANN**

# one-piece
# wonder

*Don't be fooled by the hexagon shapes that bounce across the surface of this luscious brown-and-kiwi-color throw. The quickly pieced rows are made up of a single, four-sided trapezoid pattern. Where the pattern pieces meet, one-print and two-print hexagons magically appear.*

- - - - - - - - - - - - - - - - - - - - - - - - - - - - - - - - - - - - - - - - - - - - - -

## materials

- 2⅝ yards total assorted green prints, paisleys, and polka dots (rows)
- 1½ yards total assorted brown prints and florals (rows)
- ½ yard light green paisley (inner border)
- 1⅛ yard brown-and-green floral (outer border)
- 1 yard brown paisley (rows, binding)

- 3⅔ yards backing fabric
- 66×81" batting

Finished quilt: 59½×74½"

Quantities are for 44/45"-wide, 100% cotton fabrics. Measurements include ¼" seam allowances. Sew with right sides together unless otherwise stated.

**tip** Press seam allowances in each row in alternate directions. When you join the rows, the alternated seam allowances will lock together, ensuring matching seams.

## the trick to trapezoids

Afraid of geometry? Don't let the term "trapezoid" scare you away from making this quilt. We've taken all the math out. You simply copy the pattern piece, cut out the pieces, and stitch them together.

## cut fabrics

Cut pieces in the following order. Pattern can be found on *Pattern Sheet 1*. To make a template of the pattern, see "What Are Templates?" on *page 201*.

**From assorted green prints, paisleys, and polka dots, cut:**
- 156 of Trapezoid Pattern

**From assorted brown prints and florals, cut:**
- 85 of Trapezoid Pattern

**From light green paisley, cut:**
- 8—2×42" strips for inner border

**From brown-and-green floral, cut:**
- 8—4½×42" strips for outer border

**From brown paisley, cut:**
- 7—2½×42" binding strips
- 23 of Trapezoid Pattern

## assemble quilt center

[1] Referring to photo, lay out assorted trapezoid pieces in 24 rows. When desired, match fabrics in neighboring rows to make hexagons.

[2] To join a horizontal row of trapezoids, start at one end. Referring to **Diagram 1**, layer two trapezoids with short edges aligned and ends offset by ¼". Sew together pieces; press seam in one direction.

[3] Add next trapezoid in row to pieced pair of trapezoids in the same manner (**Diagram 2**). Continue adding trapezoids until all pieces in row are sewn together.

[4] In the same manner, join pieces in remaining rows, pressing seams in one direction and alternating direction with each row (see Tip on *page 182*).

[5] Join rows to make quilt center. Press seams in one direction. Trim quilt center to 48½×63½" including seam allowances (**Diagram 3**).

## add borders

[1] Cut and piece light green paisley 2×42" strips to make:
  ▸ 2—2×81" inner border strips
  ▸ 2—2×66" inner border strips

[2] Cut and piece brown-and-green floral 4½×42" strips to make:
  ▸ 2—4½×81" outer border strips
  ▸ 2—4½×66" outer border strips

[3] Aligning long edges, join a short inner border strip and a short outer border strip to make a short border unit. Press seam toward outer border strip. Repeat to make a second short border unit.

[4] Repeat Step 3 with long inner border strips and long outer border strips to make two long border units total.

**DIAGRAM 1**

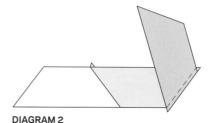

**DIAGRAM 2**

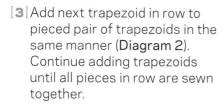

48½"

63½"

**DIAGRAM 3**

[5] Aligning midpoints, sew short border units to short edges of quilt center, beginning and ending seams ¼" from quilt center corners. Repeat to add long border units to remaining edges, mitering the corners, to complete quilt top. (For details, see Mitering Borders, *page 208*.) Press all seams toward border units.

## finish quilt

[1] Layer quilt top, batting, and backing; baste. (For details, see Quilt It, *page 197*.)

[2] Quilt as desired. Machine-quilter April West stitched an allover swirling floral pattern across the quilt top.

[3] Bind with brown paisley binding strips. (For details, see Better Binding, *page 206*.)

## color option

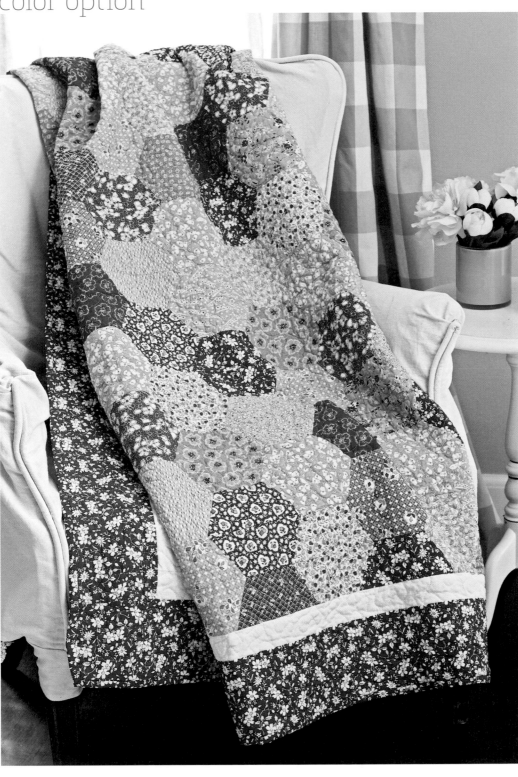

A reproduction collection of 1930s prints makes a super-size Grandmother's Flower Garden-type throw from One-Piece Wonder. Using a flannel design wall, lay out the trapezoid shapes in rows and align prints to form one-print hexagons. Surround the pieced quilt center with a solid white inner border to crisply offset the assorted prints before adding a red print outer border.

PHOTOGRAPH
**ADAM ALBRIGHT**

# color
## fun
### daisies

Brighten your day with a bouquet of daisies set off by white-and-black prints in a fast and fusible, cheery wall hanging.

DESIGNER **LINDA SULLIVAN**
PHOTOGRAPHS **GREG SCHEIDEMANN**

*To add to the whimsy of this quilt, a pieced foundation (rather than a single fabric) is created for the appliqué. The variety of prints adds interest and movement to the finished quilt overall.*

## materials

- 5—9×22" pieces (fat eighths) assorted white-and-black prints (quilt center)
- 4—9×22" pieces (fat eighths) assorted green prints (appliqués, outer border, binding)
- 3—9×22" pieces (fat eighths) each of assorted yellow, pink, turquoise, and orange prints (appliqués, outer border, binding)
- ⅛ yard black swirl print (inner border)
- ⅔ yard backing fabric
- 40×23" batting
- Lightweight fusible web
- 40-wt. cotton thread and embroidery floss: green, yellow, pink, turquoise, and orange
- 13—⅝"- to ⅞"-diameter buttons: green, yellow, pink, turquoise, and orange
- Tear-away stabilizer

Finished quilt: 33½×16½"

## cut fabrics

Quantities are for 44/45"-wide, 100% cotton fabrics. Measurements include a ¼" seam allowances. Sew with right sides together unless otherwise stated.

To make the best use of your fabrics, cut the pieces in the order that follows. Patterns can be found on *Pattern Sheet 1*. To use fusible web for appliquéing, complete the following steps.

[1] Lay fusible web, paper side up, over patterns. Use a pencil to trace each pattern the number of times indicated in cutting instructions, leaving ½" between tracings. Cut out each fusible-web shape roughly ¼" outside traced lines.

[2] Following manufacturer's instructions, press fusible-web shapes onto backs of designated fabrics; let cool.

Cut out fabric shapes on drawn lines. Peel off paper backings.

**From each white-and-black print, cut:**
- 1—5½" square
- 1—3½×5½" rectangle

**From assorted green prints, cut:**
- 2—2½×22" binding strips
- 20—1½×3½" rectangles
- 2 each of patterns D, F, F reversed, G, H, I, I reversed, J, J reversed, K, and K reversed
- 1 each of patterns D reversed, E, E reversed, G reversed, and H reversed

**From assorted yellow prints, cut:**
- 1—2½×22" binding strip
- 14—1½×3½" rectangles
- 2 of Pattern B

QUILT ASSEMBLY DIAGRAM

BACKGROUND UNIT DIAGRAM

**From assorted pink prints, cut:**
▸ 1—2½×22" binding strip
▸ 18—1½×3½" rectangles
▸ 1 of Pattern A
▸ 2 of Pattern C

**From assorted turquoise prints, cut:**
▸ 1—2½×22" binding strip
▸ 18—1½×3½" rectangles
▸ 1 each of patterns A and B
▸ 2 of Pattern C

**From assorted orange prints, cut:**
▸ 1—2½×22" binding strip
▸ 16—1½×3½" rectangles
▸ 1 each of patterns A and B
▸ 2 of Pattern C

**From black swirl print, cut:**
▸ 2—1½×27½" inner border strips
▸ 2—1½×8½" inner border strips

## assemble quilt top

[**1**] Sew together an assorted white-and-black print 5½" square and an assorted white-and-black print 3½×5½" rectangle to make a background unit (**Background Unit Diagram**). Press seam toward darker print. Repeat to make five background units total.

[**2**] Referring to **Quilt Assembly Diagram**, sew together five background units to make quilt center. Press seams in one direction. The quilt center should be 25½×8½" including seam allowances.

[**3**] Sew short black swirl print inner border strips to short edges of quilt center. Add long black swirl print inner border strips to remaining edges. Press all seams toward inner border.

[**4**] Referring to **Quilt Assembly Diagram**, sew together 10 assorted green, yellow, pink, turquoise, and orange print 1½×3½" rectangles to make a short outer border strip. Press seams in one direction. Repeat to make a second short outer border strip.

[**5**] Sew together 33 assorted green, yellow, pink, turquoise, and orange print 1½×3½" rectangles to make a long outer border strip. Press seams in one direction. Repeat to make a second long outer border strip.

[**6**] Sew short outer border strips to short edges of quilt center. Add long outer border strips to remaining edges to complete quilt top. Press all seams toward inner border.

**APPLIQUÉ PLACEMENT DIAGRAM**

**QUILTING DIAGRAM**

## appliqué quilt top

[**1**] Referring to **Appliqué Placement Diagram**, lay out all appliqué pieces on quilt top. When pleased with the arrangement, fuse pieces in place. (Linda recommends individually assembling each flower with its stem and leaves on a nonstick pressing sheet before fusing it to the quilt top.)

[**2**] Set up your machine for a 2mm-wide satin stitch. To prevent quilt top from puckering while you appliqué, place tear-away stabilizer on quilt top wrong side and pin in place.

[**3**] Using thread that matches each appliqué and working from bottom layer to top, machine-appliqué pieces. Satin-stitch a vein down the center of each leaf.

## finish quilt

[**1**] Layer quilt top, batting, and backing. (For details, see Quilt It, *page 197.*)

[**2**] Quilt as desired. The appliqué pieces and inner border of this quilt were stitched in the ditch (**Quilting Diagram**).

[**3**] Bind with assorted green, yellow, pink, turquoise, and orange print binding strips. (For details, see Better Binding, *page 206.*)

[**4**] Using contrasting embroidery floss, hand-stitch a button to the center of each appliquéd flower.

# color option

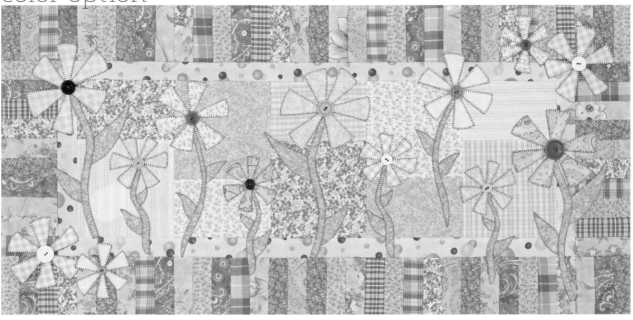

On this toned-down version of "Color Fun Daisies," a variety of blue prints were used to construct the strip-pieced outer border. To do it, join five assorted blue print 1½x22" strips to make a strip set. Press the seams in one direction and cut the strip set into six 3½"-wide segments. Repeat to make eighteen 3½"-wide segments total, then join to make the outer border strips.

tip

The presser foot must be up when you're threading most machines to ensure the thread goes through the tension discs. If stitch quality is poor, lift the presser foot and rethread the machine. Often this is the only fix you need.

# back to basics

Flip through these pages to learn the how-tos of quilting. It's all here, from choosing the best tools and supplies to finishing your project with quilting designs and binding.

# tools of the trade

*Having the right tools on hand will make quilting even more fun.*

## rotary-cutting tools

**Rotary cutters** have round blades that enable you to cut straight-edge shapes more quickly and accurately than scissors can. They come with various blade sizes—a good size for a first blade is 45 mm. Experiment with handle styles to see which you prefer.

For making perfectly straight cuts, choose a **thick, clear acrylic ruler**. A good size to start with is a 6×24" rectangular ruler marked in ¼" increments.

Always use a rotary cutter with a **cutting mat** specifically designed for it. In addition to protecting your work surface, the mat helps keep the fabric from shifting while you cut. Start with a 17×23" mat marked with a 1" grid, hash marks at ⅛" increments, and 45° and 60° angles.

## fabrics

The best fabric for quiltmaking is 100% cotton because it minimizes seam distortion, presses crisply, and is easy to quilt. Our instructions specify quantities for 44/45"-wide fabrics unless otherwise noted. We allow for a little extra yardage to accommodate minor cutting errors and slight shrinkage.

There are conflicting opinions about the need to prewash fabric. The choice is yours, but if you have any doubts about colorfastness, test the fabric before adding it to your quilt.

**tip** Blades on rotary cutters are extremely sharp. Develop a habit of closing or retracting the blade after each cut, or buy a cutter with a self-retracting blade.

## threads

For piecing and most quilting, match the thread fiber to the fabric. Because most quilters use 100% cotton fabric, 100% cotton thread is ideal. If you find your **thread breaking**, try a new spool; old thread can become brittle and lose elasticity.

## needles

The preferred sewing-machine needle for woven cotton fabrics is called a sharp. Sizes 75/11 and 80/12 are good choices for piecing, quilting, and binding most quilts. Use a smaller needle (70/10) if you're piecing tightly woven batiks and a larger needle (90/14) for flannels. Dull needles can cause **skipping or uneven stitches**, so it's a good idea to insert a fresh needle at the start of every project.

## sewing machine

Any machine with a straight stitch and well-adjusted tension (not too tight or too loose) will work for piecing. A machine that also can zigzag- or blanket-stitch makes machine appliqué possible. If your machine has **poor stitch quality**, before making any other adjustment, lift the machine's presser foot and rethread the machine.

tip  Use cotton thread for cotton quilts; the fibers will be equal in strength and should wear evenly.

# piece and appliqué

*Whether you like patchwork or appliqué,
the keys to success are practice and patience.*

## stitching

Quilting depends upon accuracy at every step. Use **exact ¼" seam allowances** throughout a quilt's construction. It isn't necessary to backstitch at the beginning of any seam that will be intersected by another seam later in the quiltmaking process. Use a stitch length of 10–12 stitches per inch (2.0- to 2.5-mm setting) to prevent stitches from unraveling before they're stitched over again. Secure seams that won't be sewn across again (such as those in borders) with a few backstitches.

## pinning

When you want seam lines to line up perfectly, **first match up seams** of pieced units. Place an extra-fine pin diagonally through the pieces, catching both seam allowances. Avoid sewing over pins, as this can cause damage to your machine and injury to you.

tip

Press seam allowances of each row in opposite directions so they abut when rows are joined.

tip

Precise ¼" seams allow you to join units, blocks, and rows with ease.

## pressing

Pressing seams ensures accurate piecing. **Set the seam first** by pressing it as it was sewn, without opening up the fabric pieces. This helps sink the stitches into the fabric, leaving you with a less bulky seam allowance.

The direction you press the seam allowance is important and is usually specified in the instructions. Typically you will press the entire seam to one side rather than open. When two seams will be joined, press the seams in opposite directions; this helps line up the seams perfectly and reduces bulk.

Make sure you are **pressing, not ironing**. Ironing means moving the iron while it is in contact with the fabric; this stretches and distorts seams. Pressing involves lifting the iron off the surface of the fabric and putting it back down in another location.

## fusible appliqué

Instead of using a needle and thread, secure cutout appliqué shapes with an iron-on adhesive—often called fusible web. Many fast-and-easy appliqué projects are fused, then secured with stitching. Follow the directions in the project instructions for how to prepare appliqué pieces for fusing.

**Choose the right fusible web.** We recommend using a lightweight, paper-backed fusible web that can be stitched through unless you plan to leave the appliqué edges unfinished. In that case, use heavyweight, no-sew fusible web. It's important to follow the manufacturer's instructions for adhering the fusible web because factors such as iron temperature, steam use, and length of pressing time vary by brand.

**Finish the appliqué edges.** A common finishing stitch for fusible appliqué is a narrow machine zigzag stitch (*see photo top right*). Position the machine presser foot so the left swing of the needle will land on the appliqué shape and the right swing of the needle will land on the foundation, just on the outer edge of the appliqué shape. For uniform machine-appliqué stitches, sew at a slow, even pace. Another common option is a blanket stitch, either by machine or by hand (*see photos center and bottom right*).

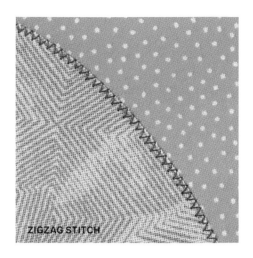

ZIGZAG STITCH

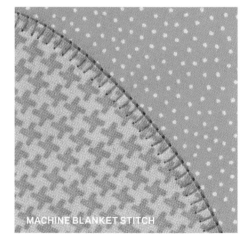

MACHINE BLANKET STITCH

HAND BLANKET STITCH

# quilt it

*Now that it's time to put it all together, consider these tips for finishing your quilt.*

## choose your batting

Batting comes in different fibers (cotton, polyester, wool, and silk), and its loft can range greatly—from $\frac{1}{8}$" to 1" or more. Generally choose a low to medium loft for hand or machine quilting and a high loft for tied quilts. Pay attention to the manufacturer's label, which recommends the maximum distance between rows of quilting. If you exceed this distance, the batting will shift and bunch later, resulting in a lumpy quilt.

## assemble the layers

Cut and piece the backing fabric to measure at least 3" bigger on all sides than the quilt top. Press seams open. Place the quilt backing wrong side up on a large, flat surface. Center and smooth the batting atop the quilt backing. Center the quilt top right side up on top of the batting and smooth out any wrinkles. Use safety pins or long hand stitches to baste all the layers together.

**tip** Always refer to the batting package label to see if the batting you're considering is compatible with the amount of stitching you plan to do on your project.

## quilt as desired

A few of the more common machine-quilting methods are shown on *page 198*. For detailed information on machine and hand quilting, consult *Better Homes and Gardens® Complete Guide to Quilting*™.

Trim the batting and backing fabric even with the quilt top edges; machine-baste a scant $\frac{1}{4}$" from quilt top edges if desired. (Some quilters prefer to wait until they have machine-sewn the binding to the quilt top before trimming the batting and backing.)

**tip** To baste layers together, work from the center of the quilt out. Pin or stitch, spacing the pins or stitches 3"–4" apart.

## stitching in the ditch

Stitch inside a seam line; the stitches should almost disappear into the seam. Using a walking foot attachment on your sewing machine will help prevent the quilt layers from shifting.

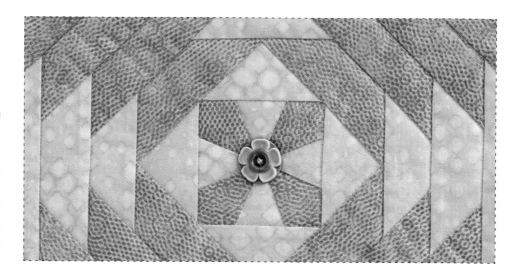

## stipple quilting

This random, allover stitching provides texture and interest behind a pattern. Use a darning foot and lower the feed dogs on your machine.

## outline quilting

Stitch ¼" from a seam line or the edge of an appliqué shape, just past the extra thickness of the seam allowance.

# quick cuts

*Rotary cutting—using a rotary cutter, mat, and acrylic ruler—makes fast work of cutting accurate fabric pieces. Here are tips for choosing and using these timesaving tools.*

[1] Choose a rotary-cutter style that fits you and feels comfortable as you press down and forward with your wrist, hand, and fingers. Ask to try out the cutter before you buy.

[2] Select the correct cutter size for your task. Generally, the more layers of fabric, the larger the cutting blade you'll need. Rotary cutters are commonly available in three sizes: 28 mm, 45 mm, and 60 mm. A good first blade is 45 mm.

[3] Use a self-healing cutting mat at least slightly larger than your fabric so you won't have to move the fabric or mat while cutting. A common standard size is 18×24".

[4] To make your fabric easier to handle, press well before cutting. If you desire a firmer hand lightly spray with starch or sizing during pressing.

[5] Hand-crease fabric folds lightly, or press them together with an iron before you cut to keep layers from shifting. Stack up to four fabric pieces together to save cutting time.

[6] Avoid stress on your arms and back by standing at a cutting table that's tall enough to let you bend at the hip, rather than the waist.

[7] Apply the same pressure on the cutter from the beginning to the end of the strip. Keeping the blade firmly against the edge of the acrylic specialty ruler, make just one steady cut from fold to selvage edges.

[8] Cut away from—not toward—your body to keep your fingers safe; make sure the blade is retracted or the guard is engaged when the cutter isn't in use.

[9] Keep a ruler from slipping by sticking small sandpaper dots or clear gripping dots (available at a quilt shop or fabric store) to the underside of the ruler.

[10] Square up the cut fabric edge after cutting three or four strips by lining up folded edge with mat grid or ruler and cutting off just enough fabric to straighten. Open an occasional strip and check for bumps or V-shapes. If you see an irregularity, square up fabric again before resuming your cutting.

tip    Practice rotary cutting on fabric scraps until you develop confidence in your cutting accuracy.

# any quilt made easy

*Quilt project look too hard? Intimidated by the number of pieces needed?*
*Use these simple hints to break down any quilt project into easy-to-sew parts.*

You can start any quilting project and successfully finish it—no matter how many pieces it contains. Enlist some of these ways to get you organized, reduce the anxiety, save time, and start you sewing now!

## sew one block at a time

You can cut, sew, and assemble most simple blocks in less than 30 minutes. Start one now, and before long you'll have enough for a few rows—or more. Breaking down a big project into small segments to fit it into your schedule is an easy way to tackle and complete an elaborate quilt.

## choose a "big block" pattern

The bigger the block, the faster it goes. Large blocks are perfect for today's bold fabric designs and colors.

## strip-piece your blocks

Cut long strips of fabric, stitch them together in alternating rows, and cut across the stitching to make sets. Sew alternating sets together, and a block is done.

## cut a while; stitch a while

Cutting hundreds of pieces all at once can be overwhelming and monotonous. Cut just enough for a few blocks, then sew them together. After you've stitched the first few, you can go back and cut some more.

## make a smaller quilt

To finish faster, select a few blocks from a big quilt pattern, sew them together, and add a border (or not) to make a wall quilt, table runner, or pillow. With a small time commitment, you'll soon have a beautiful gift or room decoration.

## chain-piece to save time

Stack paired units together next to your sewing machine. Feed the pieces under the needle one at a time, but don't lift the presser foot or clip the thread. Snip them apart later, when you're ready to press.

## repeat a block pattern

Choose a simple block—like Four-Patch, Nine-Patch, Rail Fence, or triangle-squares—and create enough for the size quilt you want. After just a few blocks, you'll click into cruise and wrap up the whole project in no time. Here's a bonus: Simple blocks are a good way to show off large-print fabrics for a great-looking quilt.

## follow the steps

Our instructions are designed to be easy to follow and to make the best use of fabric. Cut and sew each set of pieces in order. It saves fabric, and everything's ready to go when you start to sew. To stop for a bit, pencil-mark your spot. Then take up where you left off.

# what are templates?

*A template is a pattern made from extra-sturdy material so you can trace around it many times without wearing away the edges.*

To make templates, use easy-to-cut template plastic, available at quilt shops and crafts supply stores. Its transparency lets you trace the pattern directly onto its surface.

To make a template of a specific pattern, lay template plastic over the pattern and trace the solid outside edges, dashed seam lines, and grain-line arrow onto the plastic using a permanent marker and ruler. (An arrow on a pattern indicates the direction the fabric grain should run.) Mark the template with its quilt name, letter, and any marked matching points (**Photo 1**).

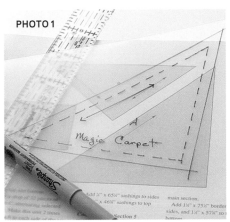

PHOTO 1

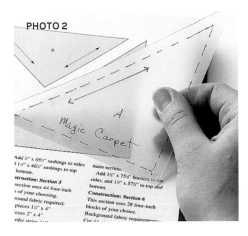

PHOTO 2

Cut out the template and check it against the original pattern for accuracy (**Photo 2**). If it isn't accurate, the error (even if it's small) will multiply as you assemble a quilt.

Using a pushpin, make a hole in the template at all marked matching points (**Photo 3**). The hole must be large enough to accommodate a pencil point.

To trace the template on fabric, use a pencil, white dressmaker's pencil, chalk, or a special fabric marker that makes a thin, accurate line. Don't use a ballpoint or ink pen, which may bleed. Test all marking tools on a fabric scrap before using them. Place your fabric right side down on 220-grit sandpaper to prevent the fabric from stretching as you trace. Place the template facedown on the wrong side of the fabric with the template's grain line parallel to the fabric's lengthwise or crosswise grain. Trace around the template. Mark any matching points

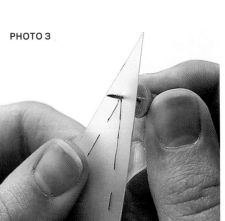

PHOTO 3

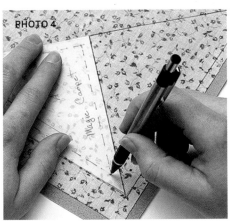

PHOTO 4

through the holes in the template (**Photo 4**). (When sewing pieces together, line up and pin through matching points to ensure accurate assembly.)

Repeat to trace the number of pieces needed, positioning the tracings without space between them. Use scissors or a rotary cutter and ruler to precisely cut fabric pieces on the drawn lines (**Photo 5**).

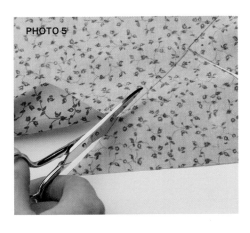

PHOTO 5

# cutting triangles

*Right triangles can be quickly and accurately cut with a rotary cutter. Learn these two common methods.*

Many quilts are made with half-square triangles (two triangles cut from one square) and quarter-square triangles (four triangles cut from one square). Some cutting directions for projects in this book will tell you to rotary-cut triangles in one of the following ways. The method you use is based on keeping the outer edges of the block on the straight grain of the fabric.

If you need to cut half-square triangles, the instructions will say:
**From light green print, cut:**
▸ 3—4⅞" squares, cutting each in half diagonally for 6 large triangles total

First cut squares in the size specified in the directions. Then line up a ruler's edge with opposite corners of a square (**Photo 1**). Cut along the ruler's edge to cut the square in half diagonally; separate the triangles. Repeat with the remaining squares. Because the triangles' long edges are on the bias, avoid stretching them when piecing to prevent distorting the seams.

If you need to cut quarter-square triangles, the instructions will say:
**From purple print, cut:**
▸ 3—5¼" squares, cutting each diagonally twice in an x for 12 small triangles total

First cut squares the size specified. Then line up a ruler's edge with opposite corners of a square (**Photo 2**). Cut along the ruler's edge to cut the square in half diagonally, but do not separate the two triangles created. Instead, line up

the ruler's edge with the remaining corners and cut along the ruler's edge to make four triangles total; separate the triangles. Repeat with the remaining squares. Because the triangles' short edges are on the bias, avoid stretching them while piecing to prevent distorting the seams.

# cutting on the bias

*Cutting on the bias is a useful technique for binding, appliqué, and sometimes piecing. Learn how and when to apply it.*

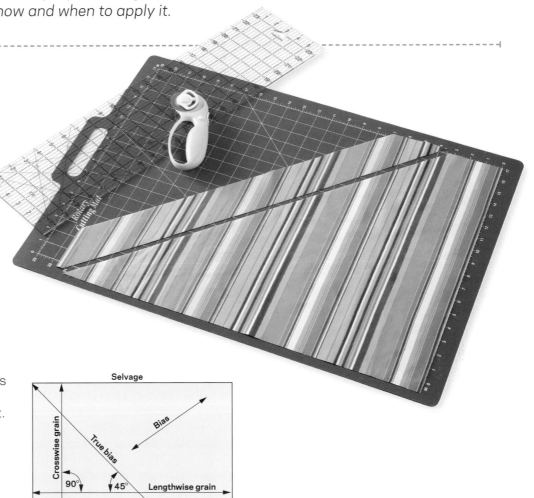

Bias runs diagonally between the lengthwise and crosswise grain line of a woven fabric. The "true" bias runs exactly at a 45° angle to the grain lines (see the diagram *below right*) and has the most stretch in a woven fabric.

## when should I cut on the bias?

Because of their built-in stretch, strips cut on the bias can be easily curved or shaped. Use them when binding curved edges or to make curved appliqué pieces such as vines or stems.

You can also cut directional fabrics like plaids or stripes on the bias for purely visual reasons. A bias binding or border cut from a stripe fabric creates a "barber pole" effect.

## how do I cut bias strips?

Begin with a fabric square or rectangle. Using an acrylic ruler and rotary cutter, cut one edge at a 45° angle. Measure the desired width from the cut edge, then make a cut parallel to the edge. Repeat until you have the desired number of strips. Handle bias strips carefully to avoid distorting the fabric.

# seams right

*Successful machine piecing depends on sewing an exact ¼" seam. Learn how to set your machine up to sew accurately.*

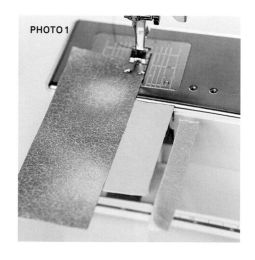

PHOTO 1

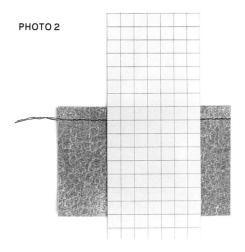

PHOTO 2

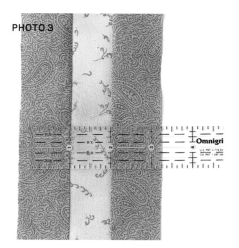

PHOTO 3

Seam guides make it easier to stitch an exact ¼" seam. The most common seam guide is a ¼" presser foot. Many machines offer this foot as an option. With this foot and the needle in the standard position, the edge of the foot serves as the seam guide.

Another seam guide option is placing layers of masking tape or moleskin on your machine bed ¼" away from the needle. When sewing, position the fabric along the tape (or moleskin) so it feeds under the presser foot and needle with an exact ¼" seam allowance (Photo 1).

Take the time to test your seam guide to make sure you will be sewing seams that are ¼" wide. Sew a sample seam with the raw fabric edges aligned with the right edge of the presser foot or up against the masking tape or moleskin. Measure the resulting seam allowance using a ruler or graph paper with a ¼" grid (Photo 2). Make any adjustments necessary to achieve the ¼" seam allowance.

To practice sewing exact ¼" seams, cut three 1½"-wide strips of two contrasting fabrics. Sew together two of the strips using a ¼" seam allowance. Join the third strip to the first two, again using a ¼" seam allowance. Press seams away from the center strip. Place the fabric right side up on a flat surface; measure the width of the center strip. If your seam allowances are accurate, the center strip should measure 1" wide (Photo 3). If your center strip doesn't measure 1" wide, you didn't sew ¼" seams. Move your seam guide as necessary and retest until you get a 1"-wide center strip.

# better machine appliqué

*Learn how to improve your machine-appliqué skills by following this guide.*

PHOTO 1

## pivoting outside curves

When appliquéing, position the presser foot so the left swing of the needle is on the appliqué and the right swing of the needle is just on the outer edge of the appliqué, grazing the foundation (**Photo 1**).

Stop at the first pivot point with the needle down in the fabric on the right-hand swing of the needle (see red dot in **Diagram 1**; the arrow indicates the stitching direction). Raise the presser foot, pivot the fabric slightly, and begin stitching to the next pivot point. Repeat as needed to round the entire outer curve.

To help you know when to pivot, mark the edges of circular or oval appliqué pieces with the hours of a clock; pivot the fabric at each hour (**Photo 2**).

## turning outside corners

When turning a corner, knowing where and when to stop and pivot makes a big difference in the finished look of your appliqué stitches.

Stop with the needle down in the fabric on the right-hand swing of the needle (see red dot in **Diagram 2**). Raise the presser foot and pivot the fabric. Lower the presser foot and begin stitching to the next edge (**Diagram 3**).

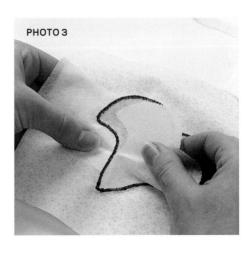
PHOTO 2

## using stabilizers

For better-looking appliqué, use a stabilizer beneath an appliqué foundation to add support and eliminate the puckers and pulling that can occur when you machine-appliqué. Remove temporary stabilizers, such as tear-away, wash-away, or freezer paper, once stitching is complete (as in **Photo 3**, where tear-away stabilizer is being removed by holding it firmly on one side of the stitching and gently pulling it away from the other side). Cut-away stabilizers are permanent and remain in the quilt or are only partially cut away after stitching. Experiment with a variety of stabilizer types to determine which works best.

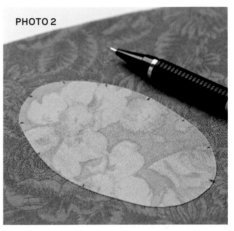
PHOTO 3

DIAGRAM 1

DIAGRAM 2

DIAGRAM 3

# better binding

*Double-layer binding is easy to apply and adds durability to your finished quilt.*

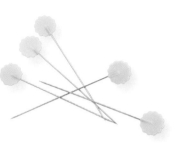

## cut the strips

The cutting instructions for each project tell you the width and number of binding strips to cut. Unless otherwise specified, cut binding strips on the straight grain of the fabric. Join the binding strips with diagonal seams (see photo *below right*) to make one long binding strip. Trim seams to ¼" and press open.

## attach the binding

With the wrong side inside, fold under 1" at one end of the binding strip and press. Then fold the strip in half lengthwise with the wrong side inside. Place the binding strip against the right side of the quilt top along one edge, aligning the binding strip's raw edges with the quilt top's raw edge (do not start at a corner). Begin sewing the binding in place 2" from the folded end.

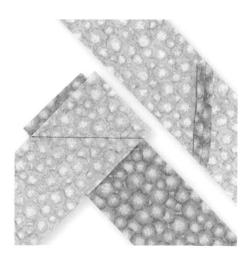

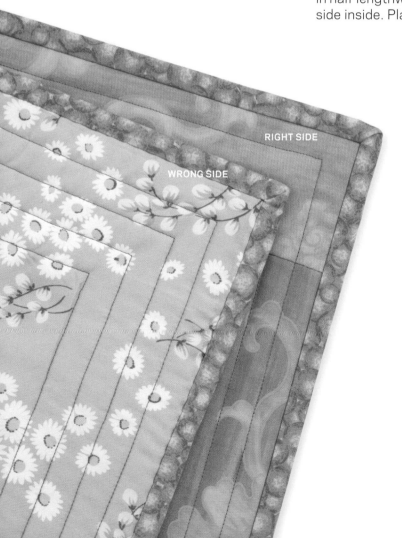

RIGHT SIDE

WRONG SIDE

**tip** Place binding strips perpendicular to each other and stitch. Trim and press seams open to reduce bulk.

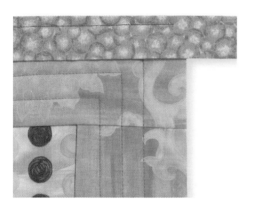

**PHOTO 1**

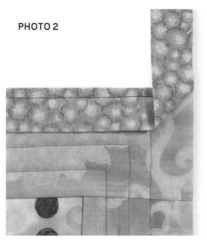

**PHOTO 2**

**PHOTO 3**

## turn the corner

Stop sewing when you're ¼" from the corner (or a distance equal to the seam allowance you're using). Backstitch, then clip the threads (**Photo 1**). Remove the quilt from under the sewing-machine presser foot.

Fold the binding strip upward, creating a diagonal fold, and finger-press (**Photo 2**).

Holding the diagonal fold in place with your finger, bring the binding strip down in line with the next edge, making a horizontal fold that aligns with the quilt edge. Start sewing again at the top of the horizontal fold, stitching through all layers (**Photo 3**). Sew around the quilt, turning each corner like this.

## finish it up

When you return to the starting point, encase the binding strip's raw edge inside the folded end and finish sewing to the starting point. Trim the batting and backing fabric even with the quilt top edges if not done earlier.

Turn the binding over the edge to the back. Hand-stitch the binding to the backing fabric only, covering any machine stitching. To make the binding corners on the quilt back match the mitered corners on the quilt front, hand-stitch up to a corner and make a fold in the binding. Secure the fold with a couple stitches, then continue stitching the binding in place along the next edge.

# mitering borders

*Mitered corners (think of these as corners on a picture frame) add a dash of drama to an otherwise plain border.*

## cutting

When our instructions specify mitered borders, cutting instructions include extra length needed to miter corners. However, if you'd like to substitute a mitered border for a standard straight border, cut strips the width (but not the length) specified. For side border strip length, measure through quilt center from top to bottom, then add twice the border width plus 6". For example, if your quilt measures 40" long and your border is 5" wide, you would cut your side border strips 56" long (40" + 10" + 6"). For top and bottom border strip length, measure through quilt center from side to side, then add twice the border width plus 6".

## preparing

If you're adding multiple borders, first join border strips for each side into a single border unit.

Fold each border strip in half crosswise; press lightly to mark centers. Fold quilt center in half in each direction and press lightly to mark center of each edge.

Pin a border strip to quilt center edge, matching the center marks and allowing excess border strip to extend beyond the corner edges. Sew together, beginning and ending the seam ¼" from the quilt center's corners (**Diagram 1**). Repeat to sew border strips to remaining edges. Press all seams toward border.

## mitering

To miter each corner, lap one border strip over the other (**Diagram 2**). Align the edge of a 90° right triangle with the raw edge of the top strip so the triangle's long edge intersects the border seam in the corner. Draw along the triangle edge from the seam out to the raw edge. Place the bottom border strip on top and repeat the marking process.

With right sides together, match marked seam lines and pin (**Diagram 3**). Beginning at the inside corner, sew together the strips, stitching exactly on the marked lines. Check the right side to see that the corner lies flat. Trim excess fabric, leaving ¼" seam allowance. Press seam open. Mark and sew the remaining border corners in the same manner (**Diagram 4**).

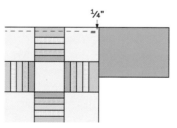

¼"

**DIAGRAM 1**

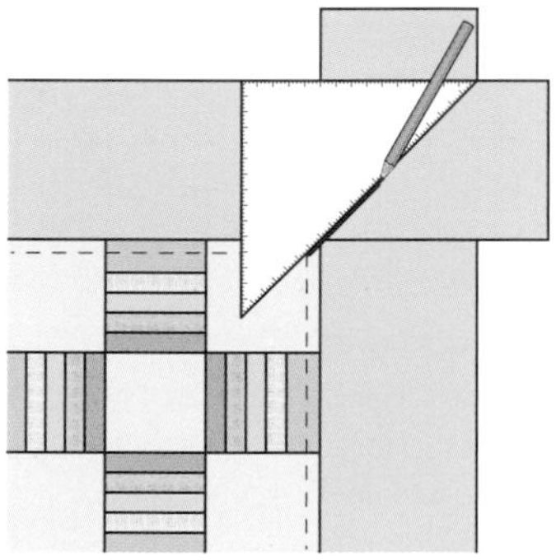

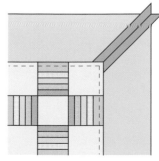

**DIAGRAM 2**

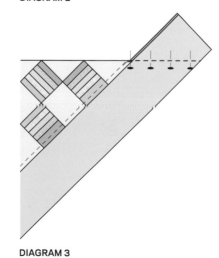

**DIAGRAM 3**

**DIAGRAM 4**